MW00606903

THE ART OF HOSPITALITY ON
LAKE MAGGIORE

Lake Maggiore and the Borromean Islands.

Sunset on Lake Maggiore.

Hermitage of Santa Caterina del Sasso.

ZACCHERA HOTELS
LAGO MAGGIORE ITALY

THE ART OF HOSPITALITY ON

LAKE MAGGIORE

THE ZACCHERA FAMILY:
ONE HUNDRED FIFTY YEARS
OF HISTORY

———

TEXT BY LUCA MASIA

RIZZOLI
NEW YORK

New York · Paris · London · Milan

Massimo, Maria Gabriella, Antonio, and Andrea Zacchera.

THE *GENS* ZACCHERA

T he Italian peninsula is an incredible treasure trove of cultural and historical wonders that the world admires and envies. Unsurprisingly, Italy holds the highest number of UNESCO World Heritage Sites, and the country is one of the most important tourist destinations in the world. To the history of humanity Italy gave Rome, and the maritime republics that led the country and the entire European continent out of the Late Middle Ages (the darkest period in the West). We also gave the world the banking, industrial, and cultural revolution of the Renaissance, well represented by Leonardo da Vinci and the Tuscan bankers, and even the Chicago Pile-1 invented by Enrico Fermi, winner of the Nobel Prize for Physics in 1938, which made it possible for nuclear reactors to exist. Not to mention Leonardo Fibonacci, who in the fourteenth century introduced Arabic-Indian numbers, algebra, and the concept of zero to the West, and Galileo Galilei, who in the early seventeenth century laid down the criteria for modern science, without which Isaac Newton and Albert Einstein's discoveries would not have existed, both of them natives of Pisa. Very few know that Galileo's father, Vincenzio, besides teaching the scientific method to his son, toward the end of the sixteenth century inaugurated the Italian melodrama *Orfeo* with music he had curated.

What's the secret of our history? It is the *gens*, the family, understood as a cooperative group that is headed by a forebear in whom it recognizes itself for its common values and traditions. It was the Etruscan *gens* that breathed life into Rome, it was the *gens* Aemilia, Claudia, Cornelia, Curtia, Fabia, Valeria who wrote the history of Rome, first as a republic and then as an empire, unifying for the first time ever both the European continent and the Mediterranean basin thanks to the aqueducts, the bridges, and the streets, as well as the gladius and the dolabra of the legionaries.

We are the land of the Medici, Visconti, Sforza, Estensi, Della Scala, Da Carrara, Borromeo, Gonzaga, Doria, Spinola, Loredan, and of the countless other families that have marked the unique destiny of our peninsula.

The family Zacchera of Baveno, on Lake Maggiore, are a fine example of this. This book describes them from the second half of the eighteenth century, when they first appear in the records as fishermen and then as timber traders, interweaving the events in their lives—made of up farsighted decisions and hard work—with those of the city of Milan. Probably, without knowing it, tracing the same path as another family, the Visconti, who were originally from Massino, not far from Baveno and Stresa, and, in the early nineteenth century, the lords of Milan as well as of most of northern and central Italy.

The Zacchera family of hoteliers from the second half of the nineteenth century celebrate the first 150 years of their activity in 2023. The *gens* Zacchera have numerous descendants, most of whom are occupied in the group's hotels located between Stresa and Baveno, on Lake Maggiore, thus guaranteeing the continuity of a family vocation that is definitely a prestigious one.

In the days when the Zacchera were fishermen and timber traders, Italy did not exist as a country but rather as a "geographical expression," as was maliciously stated by the Prime Minister of the House of Austria, Von Metternich, the champion of the Holy Alliance between Russia, Prussia, and Austria. This alliance put an end not only to the Napoleonic period, but, above all, to the yearning for freedom of the European populations who had been born in the shadow of the French Revolution. However, when the Zacchera became hoteliers Italy did exist, proclaimed as a kingdom on March 17, 1861, and later expanded to include Veneto and Friuli in 1866, and finally the entire peninsula in 1918.

The history of the Zacchera family is interwoven with that of the country. As concerns the country's historical dramas, such as the two world wars. And as concerns its environmental dramas, such as the great flood of Lake Maggiore in October 2000 that seemed to have brought the family to its knees (already badly affected by another disastrous flood in 1993). But also as concerns the spirit of innovation that allowed Italy to rise up again, each time stronger and more vibrant than before; that made it possible, starting in 1945, to embrace the incredible opportunity that was represented by the great industrial revolution that turned Italy from being a poor agricultural country into a manufacturing power, among the top ten economies in the world. Most importantly, the Zacchera family managed to grasp the opportunities offered by tourism, which on Lake Maggiore goes way back in time, but definitively took off after World War II, becoming the tourism and hospitality industry, capable of offering itself to the whole world, of hosting the entire planet, whatever language their guests speak, whatever their provenance and culture. The *gens* Zacchera in the hotelier sector owes everything to the brothers Francesco, Carlo, Dino, Aldo, and to the sisters Mariuccia and Giuseppina. Together they gave a fundamental boost to the growth of tourism for the group and for Lake Maggiore: without their foresight and their resolve the *gens* Zacchera would never have held such an important role and been as important as it is today. Very few experiences such as those of hoteliers represent the litmus test of the historical events that affect the area in which they live. Hotels are their most visible and important social and cultural landmarks, and hoteliers are the leading ambassadors of hospitality and catering services. The powerful of the earth, like Napoleon Bonaparte with his fearsome troops, rise and fall, but hotels and hoteliers remain. Hosting has been a sign of civilization from the days when strangers were welcomed around the campfire in the African savannah, sharing talk and food thousands of years ago. The verb "to host" comes from the Latin *hospes*, meaning establishing a relationship of mutual solidarity.

The Piedmont shore of Lake Maggiore has been the site of the fledgling Italian tourism industry but also of the equally young national industry thanks to the presence of water, timber, and a direct route to France along the road that climbed up as far as the Simplon Tunnel, and with the railway line that traveled through the bowels of the mountain along the Frejus Tunnel. This explains its importance in creating a tourist destination thanks to access routes, a temperate climate, the beauty of nature, and the proximity to the rich Lombard lowlands with their uninterrupted flow of wealthy vacationers.

The group of Zacchera Hotels are currently run by the siblings Antonio, Massimo, Maria Gabriella, whom everyone calls Gabriella, and Andrea, supported by their respective spouses, by their cousins, and by their historic collaborators. They are a close-knit team, with tasks that are well distributed and at the same time capable of being exchanged ("multitasking" as it is referred to today). In the footsteps of their *gens* they are projected toward the future both in terms of technology and planning, preserving at the heart of their business customer satisfaction, as well as the ability to professionally shape and individually motivate the small team of collaborators that helps them to manage that sort of diffuse company that has become Gruppo Zacchera: over nine hundred rooms spread over just a few miles, and the ability to host business meetings and provide catering for over one thousand people at the Grand Hotel Dino alone.

The *gens* Zacchera has always been particularly open to technological innovation.

In 1988 the Grand Hotel Dino was the first hotel in Italy to have a magnetic key for the rooms and an automation system. The group uses management software (ERP) that was developed in-house to be able to better answer to the needs of the unique and complex industrial reality that is represented by Zacchera Hotels. This system will be further implemented by applying the most recent advances in AI that, along with statistics and algorithms, will allow for better production planning. The conversion to digital has made it possible to save fifty trees per year, equal to around 21,000 pounds of carbon dioxide absorbed. The ISO 14001 and EMAS (Eco-management and audit scheme) certificates obtained by the group's hotels are a guarantee of its resolve and innovative environmental management.

The *gens* Zacchera are members of the Italian and international hotel elite. A membership sanctioned by the passing of time and the successes they have notched up.

Zacchera well represents this incredible treasure trove of wonders that is Italy.

Renato Andreoletti

CONTENTS

MEMORIES OF LAKE MAGGIORE

NEW TRAVELERS AT THE TURN OF THE MILLENNIUM

LET YOURSELF BE WELCOMED

Advertising poster for Baveno, Lake Maggiore, 1930s.

MEMORIES OF
LAKE MAGGIORE

T he general stood up straight on the wharf. Behind him was a small throng of people. The court of the faithful, traveling with the hero. Maresciallo Berthier approached Napoleon. They were friends. Bonaparte had made him a joint chief and he deserved credit for Italy's victory as well. The two men moved away from the group, as if to find a moment of peace after the tumult of the war. The still water of the lake, caressed by the breeze, seemed to melt the dust of the battlefield, the memory of the war. They could breathe in the peaceful morning air: the atmosphere was light, it was that of lacustrine serenity. Joséphine de Beauharnais, Napoleon's first wife, got on board the boat moored to the pier. She was followed by the others, all the way to the general.

The crossing from Stresa to Isola Bella was a short one, just a few minutes, marked by the firm strokes of the oars. Napoleon remained standing at the bow of the hull. He looked out, assessing the breadth of the lake, surrounded by mountains. Some of the peaks were still snow-capped.

On the island, the administrator of Palazzo Borromeo seemed nervous. He paced back and forth in the courtyard of the villa. He gave the servants orders, never taking his eyes off the French passenger boat that was approaching. Napoleon's unexpected arrival caught everyone off guard. The Count was on a mission at the Holy See and could not be there to welcome the guest. It was up to the administrator to defend the house. From his point of view, more than a visit, Napoleon's arrival felt like an attack. Hand-to-hand combat.

It was the summer of 1797. The island had been purchased two centuries earlier by Prince Borromeo, who dedicated it to his wife Isabella. The island's name had been chosen precisely because of the desire to offer that enchanting place to his consort. Later, again in her honor, he had planned the building of a sumptuous palazzo, as precious as a royal palace. It would take almost four centuries to complete the work; the labor of hundreds of architects, engineers, gardeners, painters, decorators, cabinet-makers. He wanted to turn a rocky spur into a place of delight: a gem set in between the mountains that were reflected on the surface of the lake.

The still water of the lake,
caressed by the breeze, seemed
to melt the dust of the battlefield,
the memory of the war.

The French boat sailed quickly along the island's massive walls, to eventually moor in a claw-shaped port. Today it is still referred to as "the grip."

The landing platform resembles a square. It reminds one of a stage set, with the painted windows of the palazzo and features that create a perspectival emotion. The search for symmetry as the heralding of perfection.

One needs to imagine the young *condottiero* as he admired the great hall of the palazzo. An astonishing hall that goes all the way up to the top of the building. A Baroque triumph on which the word *Humilitas* stands out. The humility with which man, even the most powerful of them all, must approach God. It was the word that was often used by Saint Carlo Borromeo, born in Arona in 1538, a word that later became the family motto.

Even Napoleon must have stopped before that word. He likely snapped his boots to salute; then he must have bent backward and lifted his gaze. He probably smiled, too, at the thought of the humility of the powerful.

From the hall one reached a painting gallery. A long room with specular walls covered with artworks, made by the greatest masters and arranged like the pieces in a mosaic. Overlooking the gallery was the balcony of a bedroom for special guests, it too framed in the manner of a painting.

General Berthier, Bonaparte's friend and lieutenant, had slept in that very room; since then, the gallery bore his name. Napoleon and his wife Joséphine were instead welcomed into an adjoining room, with a view of the lake. It was during that first visit that the future Empress of Italy and France fell in love with Lake Maggiore and the Borromean Islands. The harmony of places featuring a secret beauty.

After crossing the palazzo one reaches the gardens. Another panorama, but a living one this time, introduced by a gigantic camphor tree. It overlooks the lake with an amphitheater of overlapping terraces, embellished with sculptures having a specific symbolic meaning. At the center is the statue of a young man with two figures reclining on either side: they represent Lake Maggiore and its rivers, the Ticino and the Toce. At the top the unicorn, the symbol of the Borromeo, and then the fundamental elements of the universe—earth, air, water, fire—also represented by statues. All around them plants and flowers, with terraces sloping toward the lake, the Italian-style garden, the winter greenhouse. Napoleon slept just one night at Palazzo Borromeo. The following day he headed to Isola Madre for a hunting party. His wife Joséphine, of Creole origin, had once again been enthralled by the beauty of the places. She had never seen citrus plants ripen this way in the north. The colors and the fragrances reminded her of her childhood in Martinique. After that first visit she would return to Lake Maggiore without her husband's imposing presence. And like countless other travelers, along the Simplon Road that Napoleon himself had requisitioned in the early nineteenth century. A great route of communication between Europe and the Mediterranean that skirts Lake Maggiore and its villas, gardens, bodies of water, and mountains.

THE GRAND TOUR YEARS

Already at the time the Zacchera family was a part of the landscape. They lived on Isola dei Pescatori, next to Isola Bella. A strip of land with a small village overlooking the Palazzo Borromeo garden. When Napoleon came to visit, Giovanni Zacchera was probably there, fishing on the lake. Perhaps his boat had crossed paths with the French one. After him the family activity had become oriented toward transportation and the timber trade. It was an activity that compelled them to travel from the Ossola valleys to the heart of Milan, along ancient waterways. The mountains covered in forests harbored marble and granite within them as well. Candoglia marble, for the Venerable Fabbrica del Duomo, and the pink granite of Baveno. Lumberjacks and quarrymen worked above and below the surfaces of the mountains, in the forests and in the quarries. Vittore Zacchera, son of Giovanni, had been an excellent fisherman, just like his father. However, he had understood the potential of the timber trade and had begun buying trunks that were chained together and transported along the Toce all the way to Lake Maggiore. He traveled downward, exploiting the currents toward Sesto Calende, down the Ticino all the way to the bifurcation of the Tornavento, near Lonate Pozzolo. He had to get past eleven rapids before his cargo could flow into the canal and slide southward, all the way to Milan.

The barges that transported the marble for the Duomo were exempt from customs tax. Written on the freight were the words *ad usum fabricae*, hence the expression "a ufo," which still today means "a sbafo" (free of charge). Instead, Vittore Zacchera had to stop and pay before he could continue to reach the warehouse on the wharf, near Porta Ticinese. He would unload the wood, and then go back the way he had come. In mid-century an ingenious invention was introduced by Carlo Cattaneo: a horse-drawn railroad for the boats. He had called it Ipposidra, and it allowed passengers to travel up the Ticino more quickly toward Angera. During that same period Vittore Zacchera had acquired a farm overlooking the lake in Baveno. It was June 2, 1858, when, for one lira per square meter, he had signed a contract to buy the land that sloped down toward the lake, which he would then also use as a storage place for the timber. From there he would continue on to Milan. On the land there was also a small building. Aptly refurbished and enlarged it would become the Osteria Milanese, the Zacchera family's first hotel.

Engraving by Luigi Rados, ca. 1820.
Trippini Collection.

Vittore had thus transitioned the family business from fishing to trade. His son Francesco would later take it to the hospitality sector. A new way of experiencing the resources of the lake, continuing to love it and prize it.

When Vittore bought the land in Baveno, his son Francesco was living in Milan. He had previously worked as a chef at the prestigious Hotel Savoy in London. After that he had moved to the capital of the Lombardy region and was living in the Ticinese neighborhood, where his father delivered wood. A long line of water connected him to his origins, on the shores of Lake Maggiore. He was going out with a girl who lived next door, Maria Garavaglia. In 1870, when the two young people decided to marry, Vittore Zacchera gave his son the land in Baveno as his dowry. And it was on that very land that Francesco built his first hotel, with a restaurant, five rooms on the second floor, and four on the ground floor. Francesco and Maria named it Osteria Milanese, as a tribute to their city and to some of the specialities of the kitchen. It was 1873. After them, in a century and a half of life, four generations of Zaccheras were to cultivate the art of hospitality, planting roots in a single territory, from many points of view still to be explored and promoted today. A frontier land, in search of a balance between its industrial soul and its touristic vocation. A land of water, where the mountain merges with the lake. And in the middle, akin to a line that joins instead of dividing, the Simplon Road. Napoleon had it built, with the local skilled workers and Italian resources. A route of communication etched in the rock, with hundreds of bridges and galleries. The only Alpine path open year-round, conceived for the cannons and transformed into the wayfarers' route.

The idea of opening a hotel in Baveno no doubt stemmed from Francesco Zacchera's experience at the Savoy in London. But it was also the result of his awareness that the Simplon Road would bring Lake Maggiore closer to Europe. After Napoleon and Joséphine Bonaparte's visit, generations of travelers reached Italy by sailing along the shores of the lake. And indeed, almost immediately, Francesco Zacchera decided to enlarge the hotel and build a stall to shelter the horses used to pull the carriages in transit.

Three stables on the lakeshore, in a solid stone building with a barn and a large roof. There was also a large kitchen garden where his wife Maria grew vegetables for the cooking. Today, where the stable and the farmstead once were, there are meeting rooms, and where bocce ball was played there's a swimming pool, and the barn roof has been replaced by a terrace. The Osteria Milanese, from which it all began, has been transformed like a continuous flow of energy, passing from generation to generation to our own day and age.

The Simplon Road brought with it the traffic of travelers and traders. All the means of transportation were horse-drawn and the highlight of the place, in addition to the quality of the food and the availability of rooms, was the stable, known at the time as the *stallazzo*. With the first money he earned, Francesco bought portions of the woods so that he could get the raw materials he needed to build the furniture for the new rooms. Hospitality is also the expression of a circular economy: from the land to the table, a hotel is a small hamlet, the living space of a community. It welcomes people who are passing through, it listens to their stories, it shares their emotions. And as in a game of mirrors, the old trades are renewed and find new expressions, new opportunities for development. Francesco Zacchera, the chef at the Savoy of London, became the chef and host in Baveno, in the family *osteria*, or tavern. His father Vittore, a fisherman and wood trader, continued to fish to replenish the hotel kitchens and he continued to transport wooden trunks from the forest to the valley. He no longer traveled as far as Milan. Instead, he would stop at his son's house, on the lakeshore.

Traders weren't the only ones traveling down the Simplon Road and stopping at Zacchera's osteria; the young members of aristocratic families did as well, often accompanied by a chaperone who supervised their education. The trip to Italy with the goal of discovering the wonders of the arts and the landscape had become a must for the new ruling classes. There were also foreign scholars, musicians, and artists who migrated southward and spent long periods of their lives in Italy. For many, the lakeshores and the charm of the Borromean Islands were more than a fleeting moment. The traces of their passages contributed to disseminating the

COMUNE DI BAVENO

Licenza d' Esercizio *rilasciata*

a *Zacchera Francesco*

figlio di *Vittore*

nato a

per l'esercizio (1) *Osteria*

sito (2) *Baveno*

sotto l'insegna *Osteria Milanese*

Domanda presentata il *26 Gennaio 1873*

Cauzione prestata L. *50*

in

Addi

COMUNE DI BAVENO

(1) Genere del Commercio di vendita.
(2) Aggiungere: *Posto in Via o Piazza . . .* oppure: *Ambulante.*

1-9   Ditta Vercellini, Pallanza

N. 7

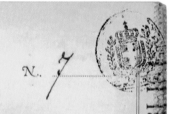

Operating license for the Osteria Milanese, which later became the Albergo Ristorante Italia with rooms for guests, and is currently the Hotel Splendid, 1873.

Dawns and dusks, gardens and historical
residences, romantic niches and castles
constituted an inexhaustible heritage of tales
that breathed life into novels and stories,
musical compositions, poems, and paintings.

beauty of the places. Writers like Dumas, Montesquieu, Flaubert, Stendhal, poets like Wordsworth and Byron, musicians like Umberto Giordano connected their very lives to the shores of Lake Maggiore.

Dawns and dusks, gardens and historical dwellings, romantic niches and castles constituted an inexhaustible heritage of tales that breathed life into novels and stories, musical opuses, poems, and paintings. It was a natural scenario and one of its backdrops was the hammering of the stonecutters working the pink granite of Baveno, the explosions of the mines in the marble quarries of Ossola. The gunpowder was transported by the women in wicker baskets; the men used wooden wedges and stone mallets to transport the slabs. It was a continuous effort of arms and muscles, accompanied by the dull sound of the hammering.

The abundance of water had also brought the first industries. There were cotton factories and mechanical workshops, textile and metalworking plants. Each activity had a typical sound: the calm of the lake was juxtaposed by the fervor of the industrial revolution that from northern Europe overlooked all of Italy.

These were also the sounds in the ears of the painters, musicians, and poets as they allowed themselves to be enchanted by the beauty of the lake. They did not seem to be at all disturbed by the throbbing industry that accelerated the rhythms of an otherwise slow existence, in harmony with nature, the seasons, the life cycles.

The Baroque splendor of Palazzo Borromeo had inspired the building of many dwellings. In Baveno, Villa Fedora had been built in the mid-nineteenth century, during the same time that the Zacchera family's Osteria Milanese was born. There were also the palaces of Sir Henfrey, the Marchesi Durazzo of Genoa, and many others. Kings and queens had also crossed the Simplon Road and stayed in Baveno.

In the summer of 1863, Ferdinand II of Portugal had stopped at the Hotel Bellevue, a building that could already host one hundred and fifty people and that was equipped with faucets for hot and cold water. The hotel was fascinating, ideal for a life of splendor and oblivion, and it would be reborn a century later in the very hands of the Zacchera family. At the time the steamboat that was used to navigate the lake was already active. The rowboats that had been used to take Napoleon to Isola Bella were no longer in use. Full-fledged ships were now available to transport the travelers and the workers from Arona to Stresa and to Baveno, to then continue toward Luino and then Locarno. In 1862, before the King of Portugal's visit, the hotels in the area had been forced to turn tourists away because the rooms were all fully booked.

The Zacchera family's osteria and stable wasn't as yet active, but a century later it would be one of the venues most involved in welcoming the Queen of England. The trip took place in 1879.

Queen Victoria, together with her daughter Beatrice and their entourage, arrived in Arona on a train from Paris. The boat was then moored in the small port of Baveno, and a carriage transported the sovereign to the castle of Sir Henfrey. The English nobleman was an engineer and an art collector. He divided his time between Italy, England, and India, where, on behalf of the British Crown, he built railroads. If the arrival of Napoleon and his court had caused quite a stir in the peace of Palazzo Borromeo on Isola Bella, the arrival of Queen Victoria, who also traveled in a reserved manner, without the clamor of an official visit, nonetheless made it necessary to reorganize the life of the town. The March 21, 1879, issue of *Voce del Lago Maggiore* reported as follows: "In Baveno the number of telegraph workers is added to, new machinery is set up, there will be a great number of Royal Carabinieri stationed there, both on foot and on horseback, and a Public Safety Representative with various guards. An infantry battalion will be stationed in nearby Pallanza, where a guard of honor will be sent to Baveno every day."

For their part, while Sir Henfrey spared no expense to make the dwelling more splendid and the park more luxurious, the townspeople offered beds in their own homes for the great number of visitors who were arriving. It was one of the first examples of a "diffused" hotel. Not only were the queen and her court visiting, there was also a constant flow of tourists coming to see the sovereigns, and before that curiosity-seekers who visited Baveno just to see what the small town was doing to welcome them. A spectacle-within-a-spectacle, whose memory remained etched in the minds of entire generations.

LA REGINA VITTORIA SUL LAGO MAGGIORE. — 1. S. M. visita i laboratori di granito - 2. e la fabbrica di spilli. - 3. Esterno della fabbrica.
4. Palo telegrafico di granito. (Disegni dal vero del signor Paolocci).

Queen Victoria of England visits the
granite workshops and the pin factory,
1879. Trippini Collection.

Advertising poster for the Società Italiana delle Strade Ferrate del Mediterraneo, 1899.

FROM THE BELLE EPOQUE
TO MOKA: ART AND DESIGN
ON THE LAKESHORE

Francesco Zacchera made it just in time to welcome the new century. He passed away in 1901, leaving his wife Maria with the task of carrying on the work. By a curious twist of fate, Queen Victoria died that same year. In the meantime, the osteria had grown and taken on the name Albergo Ristorante Italia. Also with Maria were the couple's three children: Maddalena, Giuseppina, and Annibale. The oldest, whom everyone called Lena, was a very active woman, a tireless worker. She was born in 1874, and had married a stoneworker in 1900—right at the turn of the century. The road to Feriolo was one wooden hut after another where the *picasass* used mallets to hammer the pink granite. Giuseppina was born a few years after her sister, and also married a few years after she did. She went to live in Stresa where she opened a bakery. For her entire life she also cultivated an interest in painting. Lastly, Annibale was born in 1893. He was just eight years old when his father died. Needless to say, the Zacchera family's restaurant and Albergo Italia were entirely run by women for the first twenty years of the new century. Mother and daughter worked tirelessly at their job, from dawn until deep into the night. Maddalena's nickname—Lena—was not only a term of endearment: it also described an unmistakable side of her character, her unsinkable willpower, and her resolute and determined personality.

In 1906 Annibale left for Switzerland. Upon arriving at boarding school, he wrote these words to his mother: "Dear Mother, the very same day I left home I reached Maroggia. I have already begun studying. My health is good. Please say hello to everyone and give them a kiss. Your loving Annibale."

That same year the King of Italy and the President of the Swiss Confederation inaugurated the Simplon Tunnel. One century after the road was built at Napoleon's behest, the tunnel made the journey toward Italy even smoother, bringing traders and tourists to the shores of Lake Maggiore. The Zacchera women's work for the restaurant and Albergo Italia continued to grow. The echo of the Belle Époque reached as far as Lake Maggiore. Those were the years of the first automobiles that took the place of carriages, the stars of the theater were witnessing the birth of cinema, and the winds of positivism encouraged people to think that the future was going to be better than the past.

Advertising brochure for the Grand Hotel
Belle Vue, now Grand Hotel Dino.

One century after the road was built at
Napoleon's behest, the tunnel made the journey
toward Italy even smoother, bringing traders
and tourists to the shores of Lake Maggiore.

But it was a dream destined to become a nightmare. The outbreak of World War I was heralded—akin to a modern prophecy—by the sinking of the *Titanic*. The grand passenger liner whose monumentality encompassed the fragile dream of modern man had struck an iceberg in the freezing waters of the Atlantic. The war broke out soon afterward, midway through the same decade.

Annibale Zacchera completed his studies in 1916 and was working in Turin at a metalworking plant. He was called to arms in February 1918. He never ceased writing to his mother, not even when he was in the trenches. Maria Garavaglia died that very same year, but infantryman Zacchera was not given leave to go to her funeral. He was instead ordered to continue fighting in Libya. Annibale refused, however, and the army demoted him to private soldier, forcing him to serve in Africa for one more year.

Annibale left the army in 1919. At a time that was anything but easy, in a country that was struggling to emerge from the miseries of war. The countryside was in tumult because of the farmworkers' strikes, while their counterparts in the city occupied the factories. Social tensions were transformed into civil conflicts. Annibale was lucky enough to find work in Milan, a city that both his parents had been fond of. He was hired to work for a company that imported spices and coffee. He often went to Genoa to pick up the merchandise. This gave him the business experience that would be useful to him when he returned to Baveno, to the family's hotel.

Annibale went back to living on the lake in 1921, working in the company owned by the Bialetti brothers. The two brothers hadn't as yet invented the "moka" coffee maker, but they did have a great deal of experience working with aluminum, and they had opened a metalworking factory that manufactured canteens and kitchen utensils.

The Bialetti company was one of the many small companies scattered around the region. The breathtaking beauty of the landscape continued to struggle to come to terms with the industrial soul of the Upper Verbano. The abundant water supply provided energy for the industries, and so, at the same time that the Touring Club was printing the periodical *L'albergo d'Italia* in the early 1920s, the EniChem and Montedison plants opened on the lake.

Stresa, Baveno, and the Gulf Embracing the Borromean Islands

Isola Bella dei Pescatori and, in the background, Baveno with the Grand Hotel Dino.

Palazzo Borromeo, Isola Bella.

Isola dei Pescatori at sunset.

Teatro Massimo in the garden of Isola Bella.

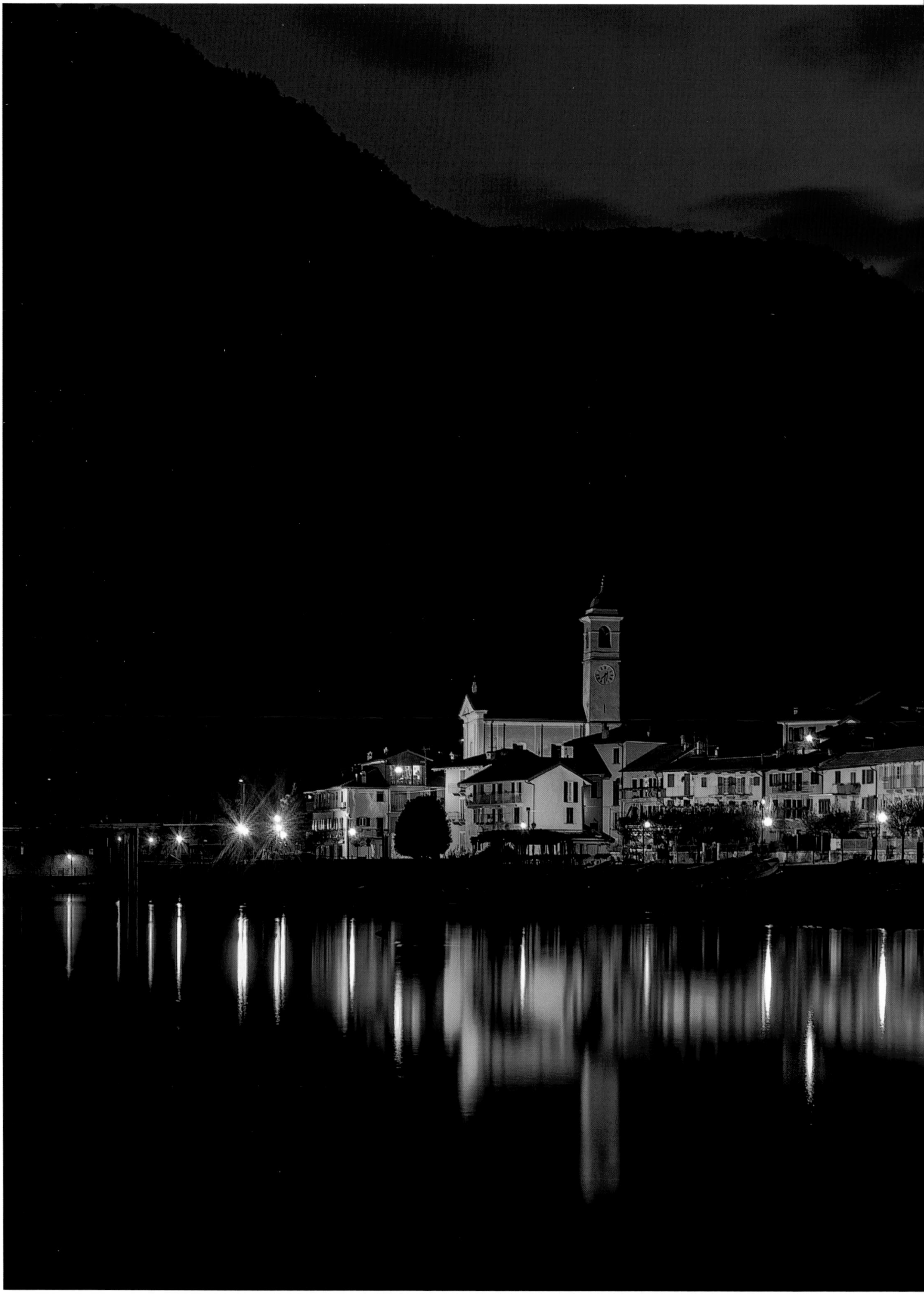

Feriolo di Baveno.

Church of San Gervasio e Protaso and Baptistery of San Giovanni (fifth century), Baveno.

Baveno.

The wharf of Baveno.

The Zacchera family's Albergo Italia and restaurant stood right there, overlooking the Borromean Islands. Its guests were the travelers passing through, the tourists, but above all the workers who would arrive every day at dawn for breakfast, and in mid-afternoon for a glass of wine and to play cards or bocce ball.

From the mid-1920s, Annibale Zacchera returned to Baveno to work fulltime for the family business along with his sister Lena.

Located next to the osteria was the park of Villa Fedora, which was inhabited at the time by the composer Umberto Giordano. The maestro was a fishing enthusiast, and he was especially keen on catching perch. He also knew a lot about good food and wine, like his friend Giacomo Puccini, who was often his guest at Villa Fedora. The two men would stroll along the lakeshore, waving their fingers in the air as though they were searching for strokes of musical genius. Guglielmo Marconi would sometimes join them. The radio he later invented aired their music.

When Annibale Zacchera and his sister Maddalena set the table in the shade of the wisteria in the garden, they often stopped to listen to Giordano playing the piano. They could tell from the touch of his fingers whether he was inspired. Sometimes they could hear him cursing, whereupon they would look at each other and smile, waiting. Soon they could hear the maestro's footsteps as he came out of the villa, crossed the park, and approached the hedge. Finally, after walking down the small path that separated the two dwellings, he would arrive in the hotel courtyard and be greeted with a smile. They invited him to sit at the table and when the delicious food was set down in front of him Giordano found his inspiration once more. When the meal was over, he often resumed waving his fingers in the air, as though he were writing a score conducted by his mind. On the lakeshore, music and hospitality came together. They created art.

During the same period the Bialetti brothers often came to visit. Annibale had remained in touch with them, cultivating their great friendship. Alfonso Bialetti had the habit of falling asleep at the table with a lit cigar in between his lips. They had worked together, and continued to exchange ideas: technical solutions

Albergo Ristorante Italia
with guest rooms in the late
nineteenth century, currently
the Hotel Splendid.

to continue improving their products. A case in point was the *lisciveuse*, a large closed tub with holes at the top and a tube. The user would put *lisciva* dissolved in water in it, mixed with wood ash. When brought to boil the steam would rise up inside the tube and then drip onto the laundry. The two men had tried it out on the hotel's tablecloths and sheets. The system worked, but then Maddalena would go to the lake and start washing everything over again from scratch. By hand, old-fashioned style, using *brielle*, wooden kneelers for the washerwomen.

In those days coffee was made by coarsely grinding the coffee beans and then infusing them directly in boiling water. Those who were more sophisticated used what was known as a Neapolitan coffee maker. The *cuccumella* was an elegant slender object: slim around the "waist," the spout was long, like the arms of a dancer. There was a tank for the water, and a filter for the coffee, which this time was ground carefully. You placed it on the flame and when the water was very hot you turned the coffee maker upside down. A dynamic gesture that required a certain skill. The coffee made like this was very flavorful.

One evening, in the early 1930s, Alfonso Bialetti arrived at the restaurant with his usual lit cigar; he was holding a strange aluminum object, wrapped in newspaper. "What is it?" Annibale had asked. "Our fortune!" Alfonso had replied.

It was the prototype of the "moka" coffee maker: a sort of miniature pressure cooker to extract coffee in a brand-new way. A revolution that would turn Italy into the home of espresso and the cradle of coffee. The Bialetti "moka" would also come to symbolize the country: a small miracle of ingeniousness, design, and craftsmanship. And it is nice to think that it was first tried out in the restaurant owned by the Zacchera family, with Annibale and Maddalena serving the first small cups in all of Italy right on Lake Maggiore.

The Milano-Laghi, the world's first highway, had just opened. Conceived and built by Count Puricelli, for many years the president of the Milan Trade Fair. The project for this major fair had been planned after the war thanks to the courageous endeavors of a handful of men who had seen beyond the destruction left by the war the spectacle of work, the growth of a new consumer society, one of trade and production. The pavilions of this first edition were the wooden shacks left behind by the soldiers of Caporetto, in the area that had previously been the theater of the 1906 World Fair. The theme of the event had been transportation. The image was symbolized by the Simplon Tunnel.

The highway was now the third chapter of the same tale linked to the great communication routes, to the transit of goods and cultures. It brought new traffic to the lakeshore: the vital heartbeat of a society where the automobile was soon to become a new symbol of freedom.

The main event in the Zacchera household in the 1920s was the wedding between Annibale and Felicina Caldera, from Castell'Alfero, a small country town in the Astigiano district filled with vineyards and master coopers. Each new season Annibale would go to Monferrato to purchase wine for the osteria. It was over the course of this travels that he met his future wife, the daughter of a farming and winemaking family.

Annibale as well produced good wine on the lake, growing and working with his own grapes. He was an entrepreneur, and he too chose the ideal life companion. Felicina would eventually become the heart of the family and of the business. A true force of nature by Maddalena's side. Both of them were tireless, the two women divided their tasks and responsibilities: one at the hotel and the tables at the restaurant, the other in the fields. They would then meet in the kitchen and on the lakeshore to do the laundry, as always using *brielle* to do so.

During the warm season the wisteria of the Italia restaurant drew the best patrons. The family's local friends, like maestro Giordano and the Bialetti brothers, but also the many tourists passing through, the traders drawn to the prospect of stopping before the Borromeo Islands, in between the historical residences and the gardens along the lake. Also rising up were many industries, but especially that of tourism. The guidebook for Lake Maggiore, published in 1925, stated as follows:

"The mild climate, the enchanting panoramas, the many kinds of excursions have attracted and still attract to the lake a vast number of people from every corner of the world. This led to the creation of another industry, that of the Hotel. And hotels have risen up almost everywhere in every place overlooking

Advertising poster for Albergo Ristorante Italia, now Hotel Splendid.

From the left, Maddalena, Annibale, and Giuseppina Zacchera outside the Osteria Milanese, later to become Albergo Ristorante Italia, and now Hotel Splendid.

The mild climate, the enchanting
panoramas, the many kinds of excursions
have attracted and still attract to the
lake a vast number of people from every
corner of the world.

the lake. On the shore almost at the same level as the water, halfway up the hills and on the highlands; hotels of every category, for travelers from big cities, for the international tourist, for those traveling for business. Besides the hotels, the villas, for families needing to get away from the humidity of the big cities, for people who wish to rest their minds and seek tranquility and rest."

Annibale Zacchera had learned his cooking skills from his father, and he devoted himself enthusiastically to the restaurant kitchen. His wife Felicina always supplied him with the best possible raw materials. The great field where the Hotel Splendid stands today sloped down to the lake and offered a huge assortment of vegetables and legumes. There were also chickens and rabbits, pigs and beehives. The hotel resembled a small farm, a modern-day *agriturismo* where the products of the land became food for the guests. Genuineness was the distinguishing feature of the Zaccheras. An indelible sign that would continue to characterize the generations to come. The warmth of a home in a large hotel.

Amid all the buzz of activity, Felicina and Annibale still had the strength to have and raise eight children. In 1926 Francesco was born. The following year Maria, called Mariuccia, and in 1929 Carlo came into the world, destined to become the figure of reference for the entire family. Corrado was born in 1931, Paola two years later, followed by Antonio in 1938. Their seventh child, Aldo, was born in 1941, while the country was at war and his oldest brother, Francesco, was graduating from hotel-management school. Giuseppina, the youngest, was born in 1944. One last pink ribbon to hang on the front door: a moment of joy just one step from the end of the war. Almost heralding the country's liberation.

Because the family was so big, it soon became necessary to make some changes to the house and hotel. The room used for the restaurant was elevated, and eight rooms were added, including two bathrooms supplied with hot water. In spite of the fact that progress was being made, in the 1920s and 1930s Italy was still rather poor, a country that was often suffocated by an archaic agricultural subsistence economy. The same could be said of the Zaccheras' restaurant and hotel. Small commodities like running water and a private bathroom could only be justified in princely villas and luxury hotels.

It is interesting to note that already back then the family was constantly reinvesting in improvements to their property, so they could offer something new to the guests in the following season. The family motto was to go forward to avoid going backward. Even a century ago the Zaccheras knew that remaining motionless meant going backward: it meant witnessing the inexorable aging of the buildings, the decline in the image.

At the end of the 1930s, at the same time that the Bialetti company was beginning to produce its celebrated coffee maker, the young Zaccheras helped their parents and their Aunt Lena with the everyday chores. There was always a lot to do for anyone who was willing. Their help was precious. In the kitchen the kids peeled the potatoes and washed the vegetables. The older children prepared the *alborelle* that Annibale fried for fifty cents a plate. When a special tool was needed the young ones would search for it in a magical part of the house they called the "emporium": a cupboard hidden behind the café counter. It contained everything: candles, light bulbs, screws, keys, and, of course, the thread with which to mend the clothes.

Clothing was handed down from the oldest to the youngest. There weren't a lot of things, but what the family had was never wasted. Everything was mended and whatever was needed was made. It was like this everywhere, but especially in the hotel that was also a house filled with life, brimming with stories. The kids would either wear sandals or go barefoot so they could run faster. All the same, their mother, Felicina, wanted them to look good whenever they went into town, and she certainly didn't want them go barefoot. She scolded them in her Piedmontese accent, something that Lena liked to tease her about. They were a lot like sisters. Two remarkable women, capable of always having the last word whatever was being talked about. Their opinions were sought out before any decision could be made. The countryside often speaks a female language, as do hospitality and care.

In the kitchen as well, even though Annibale was the cook, everyone lent a hand and some of the dishes were a group effort. For instance, rice soup, chestnuts, and milk. This was one of Felicina's specialities that the customers adored. Some of the guests were famous people, like the hero of the skies Italo Balbo. He had a home in Stresa and often stopped to eat at the Zaccheras'.

The family of Annibale Zacchera in 1938. From the left: Maddalena, Paola, Annibale, Corrado, Antonio, Felicina, Mariuccia, Francesco, and Carlo.

Annibale and Felicina Zacchera, center, with their eight children: Aldo, Carlo, Corrado, Francesco, Antonio, Paola, Mariuccia, and Giuseppina. Early 1950s.

The Zacchera brothers in the early 1950s: Corrado, Carlo, Francesco, Aldo, and Antonio.

In the fall the children would climb through the woods that rose up toward the Mottarone to gather chestnuts. They washed them and arranged them in layers in the attic, covering them with leaves. Later, they again washed them for nine whole days in running river water—this was known as the "novena." Finally, they dried them in the sun. The children also had the job of picking nettle leaves, wild asparagus tips, blackberries, blueberries, and wild strawberries. They also collected acorns for the pigs. The animals were part of the family and ate the leftovers from the restaurant. During the winter Annibale prepared the salami, prosciutto, and bacon that that was brought to the table all year.

Francesco and Carlo, the oldest boys, took turns wearing a white jacket with golden buttons, and they would stand on the street at the entrance to the restaurant to invite those passing by to come in and try the specialities of the house. All it took was a few cars and the night was a good one.

Other specialties in winter were cabbage soup, potatoes, and beans. The kitchen garden was generous. Annibale especially focused on meat and fish. Cod was always on the menu on Fridays. Thursday was tripe day. The name Osteria Milanese, which had appeared on the occasion of the Queen of England's visit, had remained in the family's memory and gave the menu a certain polish. In addition to the recipes typical of the lake, there were risotto, cutlets, and ossobuco. The restaurant had eight tables inside and just as many outside, under the wisteria. A wood oven was used and the logs were piled up outside, sheltered from the rain. The first refrigerator did not arrive until after the war, but there was a cellar filled with places where Annibale could store the wine and the room temperature remained constant through every season. It was a sort of natural icebox, and there was an endless number of steps to reach it. "How many times did I climb all the way down there!" Mariuccia recalls. "We kept everything down there, and you had to be fit to be able to come and go. That grotto was our first gym!" Today it hosts the Hotel Splendid's health club, and the restored well provides water for the sauna.

Annibale could see that his children were happy to lend a hand, even though they were still very young. This encouraged him to think about expanding the hotel.

April 25, 1945, is the date
that marked the start of peacetime.
The moment when we could start
rebuilding what had been destroyed.

Making it grow so that everyone would have a job, exploiting the talent and the resources of each one of them. All in the family, of course.

In the meantime, however, another war had to be dealt with. The Jewish families in the area were subjected to racial laws and many of them had managed to escape across the border starting out from Albergo Ristorante Italia. Information circulated in many of the locations in the area, and the hosts were often the first to know things.

Count Balbo became the Minister of Aviation and Annibale Zacchera was forced to once again don a uniform. The previous war had left a mark on him, keeping him far away from home as his mother lay dying. But as though he had a guardian angel, in 1941 his son Aldo had been born. The law favored parents who had at least seven children, lowering their taxes and exempting fathers from military service. In July of that same year, he went on leave and returned to Baveno to open a hotel and a restaurant in view of the summer season.

In the meantime, his oldest son, Francesco, had moved to Milan to get experience in the hospitality sector. He had found work in one of the properties of the Gallia family, the renowned Hotel Continental. It was a prestigious hotel right in the heart of the city. Its guests were often famous people: industrialists like Donegani, the founder and CEO of Montecatini, opera singers like Beniamino Gigli, actors and filmmakers like Vittorio De Sica. Mussolini himself had eaten at the hotel restaurant: Francesco had served him vegetarian dishes and citrus juices.

After the armistice the war became dramatic. It no longer concerned just the soldiers on the front line but all of civil society. The Zaccheras' Albergo Ristorante Italia was often used to welcome the families of the displaced who arrived there from the towns of Piedmont and Lombardy. Some hotels became military hospitals. A German command took over the Hotel Bellevue.

The raids began on September 13, 1943, right in Baveno. Fourteen people were arrested and killed. Their bodies were dumped in the water. The following days the operations continued in other towns on the lake. The victims numbered over twenty.

Regardless, people continued to live and work. Felicina would often go to Borgo Ticino by train to buy contraband goods. She continued to cultivate the kitchen garden, and added to the farmyard animals were sheep, which the kids took out to graze in a large meadow opposite Villa Fedora. Mariuccia had learned to weave and there were wool stockings for everyone in the family. The situation was destined to get worse, but fortunately the land offered the resources that were needed to survive. There was a kitchen garden and there were animals, fish in the lake, the wood in the forests. The children had grown increasingly independent and they would go the mountains and cut branches to bring back home. What had once been their great-grandfather Vittore's activity had been passed down to the children, who used a cart to transport the heavier logs. The trunks were instead transported by horse-drawn carts to the road where they were sawed. Always by hand, always by the younger members of the family.

Mariuccia finished her studies while every morning Carlo went to school in Stresa by bicycle. He fitted solid tires so there was no chance of a puncture. He would often find himself in the crossfire of the partisans and the Germans. Leaving the house became more dangerous each day.

In September 1944, the airplanes of the Allied air forces had machine-gunned and sunk two boats used on the lake, causing dozens of civilian victims. Just prior, in the month of June of the same year, there had been the massacre of Fondotoce: forty-three partisans had been shot dead. Right after that there had been an action of the fighters of the Mottarone at Baveno station. During a shoot-out two officers from the occupation troops were killed, probably among those responsible for the massacre. The retaliation was ferocious and immediate. The following day raids were carried out, and Francesco Zacchera, who was at home with the flu, was captured along with fifty other people. He was accused of draft-dodging. Miraculously, he managed to save his skin, thanks to the help of his brother Carlo and his father Annibale, who went to the military command with a medical certificate. Instead, seventeen young partisans who had escaped execution at Fondotoce were taken to the square of the pier in Baveno and shot dead on the shore.

April 25, 1945, is the date that marked the start of peacetime. The moment when we could start rebuilding what had been destroyed. At the Zacchera home the first thing that was restored was the garden. Then a large veranda was built, and the interior of the hotel was renovated. Almost symbolically, the National Liberation Committee installed itself at Villa Fedora, where Umberto Giordano had composed many of his most famous arias.

The first coffee machine was installed in the café-bar and soon afterward a refrigerator was added. While it did not replace the underground icebox that the children referred to as "la grotto" (the cavern), it did bring with it an air of efficiency and modernity, and it also cut down on the hard work that had to be done previously. Francesco also had professional experiences on the lake during the war. He worked at the Hotel des Iles Borromées in Stresa, and then at the Hotel Milano, also on the shores of Lake Maggiore. In the end, he had gone back to working at the family hotel, where he was sure he could contribute what he had learned. But it was especially Carlo, his younger brother, who helped their father Annibale to run the family business. Carlo spent more and more time in the office, studying the laws, observing the competition, drafting contracts, and exploring new markets. The Zacchera family's business had arisen from an intuition and it had been pursued tenaciously, passionately, with devotion, and a willingness to make sacrifices. It was not a job, it was a way of life. The hotel was like a house, just bigger. Welcoming patrons was like receiving guests: people who were always in some ways special, to be looked after with care and attention. The company was founded on a circular economy where nothing is created, and, above all, nothing is destroyed. Everything is transformed, like energy. The positive energy of a life that is well worth living.

THE ECONOMIC BOOM AND
THE CULTURE OF TOURISM

The postwar period in the Zacchera household started with a blessing. It was a warm day in May 1946. The waters of the lake glistened in the sun and it was pleasant to eat outside, under the wisteria. A large, long, dark American car had arrived. A Cadillac. The license plate was odd, of the kind that had never been seen before around those parts. Behind the wheel was a driver in uniform. After parking the car he came out and opened the back door. A solid-looking, heavyset man emerged. His face was round, his gaze peaceful, and his eyes sharp. He might have resembled a farmer if he hadn't been wearing a cassock, a cross around his neck, and a purple sash around his waist. He was undoubtedly an important man of the church who instilled a great amount of respect.

Carlo Zacchera got up the courage to go over to the two men. He already possessed the art of hospitality, so he knew exactly what to do. The high prelate also wore a bizarre hat with a wide brim and a rounded top. The young ones thought he looked like Saturn, encircled by rings, the way they had studied it in school. With a smile he pointed to the garden. Carlo set the beautiful rose granite table in the shade of the vine for him. The driver instead stayed inside, eating in the dining room. The distance between the two men only caused the mystery to grow. Carlo went from one to the other, without forgetting the other patrons waiting to be served. Between one dish and another, something the driver said about the horrible conditions of the road after the war told Carlo they came from Paris. The Peace Talks had just taken place and that man was Monsignor Roncalli, the papal nuncio. While De Gasperi was overseeing the difficult conditions of a country seen as a traitor by the vanquished and as an enemy by the victorious, the nuncio had carried out some crucial diplomatic activity. Ten years later, in 1958, he would become pope. They would call him the Good Pope, and he would eventually be canonized.

But that midday in May 1946, he was thoroughly enjoying Lena's handmade pasta, the perch fillets grilled by Annibale, the white bread baked at home by Felicina. Mariuccia had gone to the cellar to get him some red wine and he had liked that too. It warmed the soul, made one feel like living, and nurtured hope. That man of the church who was used to talking to God understood men. And in all the fervor of the activity that accompanied the meal at the Zaccheras' he had seen an entire country. There was the flavor of the midday with the tolling of the bells in the background: the young people busily coming and going from the kitchen, the workers finishing their shifts in the factory, and the stonecutters who washed their hands covered in dust from the granite and the marble before sitting down to eat. It was a slice of Italy that looked with confidence to the future.

When, at the end of his meal, he got up and blessed everyone there, before him was the image of a country that would, by working hard, find the way to get back up and grow, eventually becoming a world economic power. Monsignor Roncalli's blessing marked the Zacchera family's day, and many others after that. Through thick and thin.

In the winter of 1951, while all of Italy was involved in the reconstruction, Annibale Zacchera decided that it was not just important to forge ahead but to look upward as well. And each time he looked at the great meadow that sloped down toward the lake next to the hotel, he imagined a new building with several floors, capable of welcoming more and more guests. It would be called Nouvel Hotel Italie, in French, which was very much in style at the time, suggesting that it was an elegant construction. Twenty-eight rooms arranged over two floors that flanked the old Albergo Ristorante Italia.

The idea was to elevate the family business to a higher level. Even the building of the hotel itself was mostly the work of the family; each time the elder brothers went out they would take off the uniforms they wore in the restaurant and don their workers' coveralls. There were lots of tasks that the builders were happy to let them do, from small demolition jobs to painting. Corrado carefully oversaw all the building phases. He was twenty years old and particularly good at working at the building site. His younger brother Aldo followed him around like a shadow. He was just a child, but he had the good fortune to be able to play at building things with him, seeing how dreams are made, brick after brick.

The work never seemed endless, there was always something needing to be done. And as soon as you stopped you started thinking about the bank debts, fearing that you might not make it. But during the first postwar years those who were

From that first season onward,
each year work would be done to
improve what was already there, a
project to shape a new dream.

willing to roll up their sleeves knew they weren't alone. Each time they raised their head to dry the sweat on their brow they would look around and see so many other people bent over their jobs. The whole country was crossed by a positive energy.

Sometimes the family would feel as though all had been lost, when the dust from the building site penetrated their bones, the same way the humidity did when it rose up from the lake in winter. It seemed as though things would never be the same again. And instead, as early as the spring of 1952, the hotel was ready. The summer season was excellent and the following year the family won the Ente Nazionale per il Turismo Award for having built the first hotel on Lake Maggiore after the war. There was reason to be proud of that prestigious acknowledgment. It was proof of the entrepreneurship and courage of the Zacchera family, their natural tendency to always look ahead.

From that first season onward, each year work would be done to improve what was already there, a project to shape a new dream. It was an idea of development that always looked to the future as something that belonged to the present.

The growth of the business also went beyond Italy's borders. On several occasions, Carlo and Francesco went to England to learn the language, and in the early 1950s they began traveling around Europe to introduce the hotel to the major travel agencies. One of their best clients was a Flemish man who organized trips "with the scent of the Borromean Islands." The tourist groups left from Brussels and reached Baveno by way of Basel. These were prize trips for the salesgirls who worked at Belgium's department stores. There was also a Swiss agency that took the tourists to Lugano by bus. A collaboration that would last forty years and that continues today with American tourists.

Leisure and work became merged into one single thing. Everyone did everything, and there was always room for those who wanted to do or learn things. The hotel was the home, the patrons were the guests.

Francesco, the firstborn, carved out a role for himself in public relations, as he enjoyed embodying the image of the hotel and of the family outside. Corrado was the man who oversaw the building, a brilliant, tireless, domestic architect.

He followed the new projects with passion and with the same enthusiasm he supervised the maintenance. He had the rare gift of understanding how things worked. He would look at them, understand them, and then fix them.

Carlo instead was taking the place of his father Annibale in the strategic management of the business. He was the one who always took care of everything and had a clear vision of the future. He slept only a few hours each night, and devoted all his energy to his work. From the administration to the restaurant, from the rooms to the suppliers, from the banks to the clients, not a single department escaped his attention. Annibale, for his part, watched the family and the business grow. He witnessed that spectacle with satisfaction, continuing to act as the patriarch of a growing community where generations crossed and aspirations grew.

Over the course of the 1950s, the drive toward modernity was still accompanied by archaic activities and customs. The first electrical appliances had been invented, and yet sheets were still washed on the lakefront. Everything was done by hand, even at the bank all the calculating was done by hand, and contracts were written up with a fountain pen in the finest handwriting. It would not be long before man would travel to space, using chalk and a chalkboard to calculate the trajectories of the spaceships.

And so, in balance between past and future, the Zacchera family built the Hotel Splendid, joining the old Albergo Ristorante Italia and the new Hotel Italie. Then, in 1957, they threw themselves into a new project and purchased the Hotel Simplon, also in Baveno. It was a marvelous piece of architecture with almost seventy rooms and 215,000 square feet of park area near the glorious Hotel Bellevue. The family built a new wing for the hotel with twenty-five rooms and two elevators. In those days, having to go up and down stairs every day was considered hard work, and the novelty of the elevator was truly worthy of note. The pope's blessing was clearly still bearing fruit.

A Crown of Valleys
to Experience Nature

Valle Antigorio. The church of San Gaudenzio in Baceno.

Valle Anzasca. Macugnaga.

Valle Bognanco.

Formazza Valley. Toce Falls.

Antrona Valley. Cavalli Lake in Cheggio.

Vigezzo Valley. Vigezzina Centovalli Railway Line.

Alpe Veglia and Devero Alp Natural Park, Lakes of Sangiatto.

Vigezzo Valley. Sanctuary of the Madonna del Sangue, Re.

Carlo was the strategic mind of the family. When an important decision had to be made, he was the one that everyone looked to.

Unfortunately, not long afterward twenty-year-old Antonio Zacchera died of pneumonia. He had suffered during the war and had never fully recovered. For the family his death was terribly painful, and they tried to overcome it with the warmth that came with new affections and by working hard. And so, in the early 1960s, Mariuccia married the *maître* of the Hotel Splendid, Giancarlo Fortina, while her brother Carlo was joined in matrimony with Margherita Silvera, a girl from Sesto Calende who was also the daughter of hoteliers. Her arrival was like a new flower blossoming on the lakefront. A flower that was anything but fragile, Margherita had a strong, determined personality. The two weddings were celebrated in the hall of the Hotel Splendid that served as a backdrop for a ceremony that was exclusively a family event.

New unions also led to new births. Joys that anticipated other sorrows. Annibale Zacchera passed away in 1963, just in time to see his grandchildren take their first steps. He was active to the very end, however, planning the purchase of a hotel in Pallanza. His death caught everyone by surprise. Francesco had accompanied Aldo to London so he could study there. They both rushed back for the funeral. The absence of the man who had been the family's guiding light left a void that was hard to fill. Francesco and Carlo, the older brothers, were responsible for taking over for him. But they were not alone. Corrado managed all the building and maintenance works; Aldo was growing and following in his footsteps. And then there were the women in the family, all of whom were remarkable. Felicina continued to be the heart of the family's domestic life, keeping everyone together, and never missing a thing. Maddalena was older now, but she was still sharp and active. Mariuccia and Margherita both just had their first children, but they continued to work. All of the generations came together in the same great house that also included two hotels. The first in a chain of hotels.

The family's most important decision after Annibale's death was its purchase of the Hotel Bristol in Stresa. The hotel featured about a hundred rooms and it was in a strategic, rather prestigious location. Originally, it had been a historical home, with a huge park, a garden overlooking the lake and the wharf. Its name

FAÇADE VERS LE LAC

Advertising poster for the Hotel Simplon, Baveno.

was Villa Mercedes, and although after the the war it had been transformed into a hotel, many continued to call it by its old name.

Annibale had dreamed of doing something like this, but he had never succeeded in finding the right opportunity.

Purchasing the Bristol was not simple, however. The owners had been involved in a bankruptcy and the property was at the center of legal disputes. Once the legal problems were resolved, the hotel was refurbished with the addition of some important new elements: a small building for the staff and new rooms for the guests. Francesco was involved in managing the hotel in Stresa together with his sister Giuseppina and with Margherita, Carlo's wife. In the meantime, Aldo had gotten married and he, his wife Teresa, and his sister Mariuccia managed the Hotel Splendid. As always Corrado was in charge of construction and maintenance. He was also involved in acquisitions for the three hotels.

Lastly, Carlo became the manager of the Simplon, where he lived with his family. When the hotel was closed, they all moved to the building opposite the Splendid, which the kids called "the winter home." But the rest of the year they lived in an apartment inside the hotel. This solution meant that they had to move twice a year. There was a small kitchen, a small dining room, and there were two bedrooms. Their parents slept in the master bedroom, while the four children all shared the same room with two bunk beds. "There was only one bathroom, so there was a lot of standing in line in the morning," Antonio, Carlo and Margherita's firstborn, still remembers. "It was strange to have a hotel completely at your disposal and still have to live in a small space. But for us it wasn't just a home, it was our life. The life of the whole family."

Carlo was the strategic mind of the family. When an important decision had to be made, he was the one that everyone looked to. And Carlo—Carlin, to those closest to him—never backed out. He had already developed the ability to think and to do, to see far ahead; this was combined with a deep humanity and concern for people and for things. He never had any time, and yet he always managed to find some to do everything, whether it involved signing a deal or listening to a collaborator. All the brothers stood together with him; they would discuss things

Advertising poster for the Grand Hôtel Bellevue, now Grand Hotel Dino, Baveno.

but without ever being divided. They found a way to resolve every matter. Working with the members of the Zacchera family gave one a reassuring feeling of protection. There was the awareness that inside that small world, inhabited by so many people, any problems could sooner or later turn into opportunities.

Paradoxically, the closeness of the family was about to be strengthened by a new sadness. The births in the 1960s of Carlo's, Mariuccia's, and Francesco's children were overshadowed by the loss of Corrado, known to everyone in the family as Dino. The Hotel Bellevue in Baveno had recently been put up for sale. It was the one that as early as the nineteenth century, when the King of Portugal came to visit, had hot and cold running water for its patrons. The Zacchera brothers had thought of buying it so they could make a further qualitative leap. They had begun negotiations and Dino was on the front line, dealing with a project that would require important construction work. For some time he had been suffering from kidney problems, but in spite of his illness, he was strong and maintained a tenacious hold on life. He drove a white Ford Cortina, a long car that looked like something out of an American movie. Whenever he went to the suppliers to purchase things for the restaurants, he liked to take his nephews and nieces along with him. He would fill the car with the kids; going places with Uncle Dino was always a celebration for them. He had to undergo dialysis on a regular basis, which was dangerous because of the risk of contracting a blood infection. It was also a long and ongoing procedure that made him feel very tired. The taxi driver who would take him to the hospital—after the procedure he couldn't drive back by himself—had become his friend. He would accompany him to the Melegnano unit, and Dino would return to the lakefront totally worn out. To alleviate his suffering, the family had donated the medical equipment that was required for dialysis to the Borgomanero hospital that was located much closer. The doctors suggested Dino get a kidney transplant, however, and the best place for that type of operation was the hospital in Zurich. The family was very concerned, but it also had a great deal of confidence in medicine and scientific research. Carlo was very close to his brother, and when it came time to decide whether or not to

Everyone in the family was working full time,
each of them doing what they were best at.
Work was one thing there was plenty of.

undergo a transplant it was he who especially helped him to feel confident. And so, once the decision had been made, the wait began. Every week, on alternate days, Dino went to the hospital in Borgomanero to undergo dialysis, while at the same time waiting for a phone call from Zurich.

Finally, on the night of March 12, 1971, the phone rang. A compatible kidney had become available. The surgery would have to be performed the following day. The brothers hopped in the car and drove Dino to Zurich. He sat silently in the back seat. His head was tilted to one side and his eyes were closed, but he wasn't asleep. He clearly felt that things were not going to go well. Sadly, he kept saying that he'd never go home again. Carlo was sitting in the front, as if leading the expedition. He told his brother to stop saying such foolish things. Carlo had a natural talent for reassuring people and for being the go-to person, whatever the situation might be. And when it came to his brother's kidney transplant, he had no doubts. Fears yes, doubts no. He knew it was the right thing to do.

Unfortunately, however, Corrado did not survive the operation. He died during the surgery and all that was left was the pain. The memory of Dino repeating the words: "Try always to love one another."

Carlo felt the weight of that death on his shoulders, as if the decision had been his and his alone. As if he had been the surgeon operating on his brother. There was no human error, nor were wrong decisions made. Life chooses to write its own story and decide for itself. Individuals can try to change the course of the events, but often all they can do is accept things, without expecting to understand them. The family came together in the memory of Dino. The day of the funeral Carlo chose a black tie; he wore it over a white shirt. After the loss of his brother he always wore a black tie. The memory of Dino's death would be with him throughout his life.

After that loss, Carlo, Francesco, and Aldo became very close; it was if they were a single person. They were like a block of pink granite from Baveno: hard, compact, impossible to scratch. And yet beautiful. Out of respect for Corrado's last wishes, they promised to love one another always.

Naturally, the negotiations for the purchase of the Bellevue slowed down. The Zaccheras asked for enough time to be able to mourn their brother's passing, but the owners would not budge from the agreements that had been made before the tragedy. There was a great deal of discussion and the mourning period had to be shortened. Once again it was necessary to decide whether to go ahead or to let things go. And once again the Zaccheras decided to press ahead. Carlo was thinking of buying the hotel, demolishing it, and then building it over again from scratch, according to a brand-new plan. Not just for Lake Maggiore but for all of Italy. They decided to name the new hotel after Dino, in their brother's memory.

The family acquired the Bellevue, and it was the start of a human and entrepreneurial adventure that would last nearly fifteen years. For Carlo the task was a personal challenge and he devoted himself to creating an imposing new structure. Each day, even when nothing was going on, something happened. The Grand Hotel Dino was always at the heart of what everyone was busy doing, even though there were three other hotels to run.

The first obstacle that had to be overcome was the approval of the projects. With great patience, Carlo would travel to Turin every week to petition the technical expertise that was needed to open the building sites. There was always some problem, always something that needed to be done over again. The plans would then become lost in the various offices, they would get mixed up in the heaps of other documents. But Carlo never gave up. Armed with his polite but firm manner, he would arrive there early in the morning before the managers did. He would ask that the papers be approved and signed, he would listen carefully to the new comments, and the following week he would return with the changes. He never felt demoralized. Neither his children nor his collaborators ever heard him complain about the institutions, not even when the State seemed to be very far removed from its citizens. An inner force seemed to be helping him put up with everything, as if the results had somehow been announced.

And so, in the late 1970s, work to demolish the old Hotel Bellevue in Baveno began. To make up for lost time the hotel was torn down in just one week, which was followed by its reconstruction. The work would last for almost a whole decade.

Carlo's idea was to build a huge American-style building on Lake Maggiore, with meeting rooms featuring large windows, a fundamental element for MICE marketing today. Carlo had never seen one. He had never been to the United States, and he had never taken part in an actual international meeting. But he had the ability to picture the future, while everyone else only had eyes for the past. Formulating long, racing thoughts, looking way ahead even if his natural horizon was surrounded by the mountains reflected in the lake. Carlo read a lot, and he thought even more. He knew how to dream about things. He could already envision them even when they were just ideas or even just the hints of ideas.

Until just a few years before, when he was just a young man, he would stop customers on the main road outside the Ristorante Italia, wearing a white jacket with gold buttons. The days of intercepting individual travelers was over: now it was time for entire companies, for organizing events, medical conventions, the presentations of new products, and sports events. While all this was going on, the management of the Simplon and Splendid hotels in Baveno, and the Bristol in Stresa continued.

Everyone in the family was working full time, each of them doing what they were best at. Work was the one thing there was plenty of. Growing up in the shadow of the three Zacchera brothers were the children from the next generation. Especially the children of Carlo and Mariuccia, who were more or less the same age. Carlo was the central figure in the family and his children saw him working in the hotels and in the office all day long, and often at night. The young ones were never asked to carry out a task, they were never forced to work. It was natural for them to follow their elders' example. "Sometimes we had our sports bag ready to go play soccer when we realized they needed us," Massimo Zacchera recalls today. "So we'd push the bag behind the curtain, don our uniforms, and go lend a hand in the restaurant or behind the counter." When there was an important event in one of the hotels, Carlo would sign his children out of school early so they could replace the waiters from other venues, who would then go where they were needed. If things ended early there was always time for a soccer match or a bike ride. But only *after* everything was finished, never before.

A NEW WELCOME
ACCORDING TO TRADITION

The project for the Grand Hotel Dino was shaped around an essential idea: to bring the meeting rooms out into the daylight. Carlo's insight was focused on the creation of a place that would be devoted to meetings and company events. He saw that new way of communicating as a great development for the hospitality sector as a whole, which until then had existed in Italy in relation to leisure time activity. The few meeting rooms that did exist in the hotels were located in the basements, or in places off to the side that were lacking in natural light. Hotel Dino would revolutionize that ancient model, and on the lakeshore it would be truly unique.

Still today the abundance of modular rooms with soundproof movable walls and large windows overlooking the lake is the fundamental resource for a structure deemed to be technologically advanced. Francesco and Aldo had shared Carlo's vision, even though everyone was in a hurry to finish the work so they could see what would happen afterward. It wasn't easy to imagine a future that was so different from the past, to think that such a big hotel would always be filled with events and guests.

Every day on the building site there were problems to solve, and over the course of the decade, the groundwork had been laid for the handover to the next generation. The three Zacchera brothers were always united when things needed to be fixed. However, Carlo always had the last word, as if there were an unwritten family pact among them that they shared nonetheless. His younger brother Aldo adored him and trusted him completely. He was always the first to act. His big, solid figure could be seen emerging from the dust surrounding the building site. "He never held back," is how Antonio Zacchera describes his uncle. "In work and in life. He was a brave soldier, always on the front line risking his life for everyone else." Francesco was the oldest. He had worked in some big hotels and was particularly good at public relations, especially dealing with clients. He was a kind, polite man. Should a problem arise, he would stay calm and confide in his siblings.

Only once did one of the three brothers make a decision by himself, when a projecting roof that ended up being too low was made for the entrance to the new hotel. It left no room for the buses to get through and Aldo was infuriated.

The building of the platform roof in front of the Grand Hotel Dino, second half of the 1980s.

The building of the Carlo Ballroom at the beginning of the 2000s.

He took a mallet and started knocking down the structure while it was still drying. "He was right, though," Antonio Zacchera admits today with a smile. "If we hadn't rebuilt the roof so that it was higher up by almost five feet, today the buses wouldn't be able to get through." The construction workers finished demolishing it and then made it over again from scratch exactly the way Aldo wanted it.

The building of the Grand Hotel Dino was an adventurous journey, also because taking shape in the construction sites was a project that Carlo alone envisioned clearly in his mind. He knew that if he presented the planning authorities with the finished plans the job would never get done. So he advanced by small steps, one construction after another, starting the bureaucratic process over again from scratch each time. Even his rapport with the architects was a special one: he would make sketches on sheets of paper and then let the specialists interpret his visions. After that he would step in, make alterations, make improvements.

Each organizational matter concerned him directly. He did a huge amount of work, as if he embodied both the father and the brother he had lost.

Every now and again it was frightening to even think what might have happened if he had been the one to leave the family before his time. But these were passing fears, shadows that faded away instantly. The hard work left him breathless and left him with little time to reflect. Thinking fast and acting even faster and effectively were things that Carlo Zacchera was very good at. By staying close to him everyone learned how to stay apace.

When it came to the basic questions, as already mentioned, the three brothers were like one, and much bigger than the three of them put together. Their individual faults faded away, eventually disappearing, while their qualities instead were added together and multiplied. Toward the end of the 1980s, when the works at the Grand Hotel Dino were almost finished and the building was ready to be inaugurated, it seemed like a lifetime had gone by since the decision had been made to purchase it.

Carlo's children were all born in the 1960s, and Antonio, the oldest, was finishing his economics studies in Milan. Naturally, after spending his childhood and his teenage years in the hotel, the company was in his heart. He had

When it came to basic questions,
as already mentioned, the three brothers
were like one, and much greater than
the three of them put together.

inherited his spirit of observation from his father, the ability to imagine the future and to work tirelessly to make it all come true. When he returned from college, he went to see the building site. He was surprised to discover that the doors to the rooms had been fitted with traditional keys. He tried mentioning magnetic key cards, but the technology was still very recent, and to install them all the walls in the rooms would have to be broken. Francesco changed the subject, Aldo pretended he hadn't heard him, Carlo invited him to continue. Antonio explained that a magnetic key card for each of the rooms would simplify the welcome phase for the guest; it also meant having all the rooms under control. Carlo had discussed it with a major hotelier in Milan who was thinking about renovating his hotel by adding digital technology. Although it might seem hard at first, it would eventually make everyone's job easier. Antonio was convinced that having remote control access was not just a whim; rather, it was absolutely necessary when having to manage a hotel with hundreds of rooms. The first thing to do was install the magnetic keys, then it would be a good idea to cable the rooms so that they could be controlled remotely: that way they could make sure that everything was in order, from the lights to the TV, from the fridge to the air-conditioning. Aldo would hear nothing of it and was absolutely against it, while Carlo accepted the idea. What he had in mind was a hotel that was especially addressed to the professional world, and he knew that technology would be an essential part of what he had to offer.

When the work first began, computers were in their early stages and everything was still done by hand. But the times they were a-changing, and the new site risked already being dated by the time it was born. With his father's support, Antonio perfected the project and personally oversaw the installation of magnetic key cards. To be able to do so the work crews reopened the building site and began breaking holes in the walls around the doors to the rooms. A box was installed that served to control the inside lighting remotely as well. If the windows were opened, special sensors on the windows automatically blocked the air-conditioning. Lastly, those at the reception desk knew whether the guest was in the room. Everything was carried out with the utmost care and skill. It was already a huge deal for those days.

In May 1988 the first block of the Grand Hotel Dino was inaugurated with a world convention of pneumologists. The hotel opened the following spring. It was a "smart" hotel featuring a series of technological innovations that were unique for those days. In actual fact, not everything worked immediately. Antonio can still remember his uncle's wry smile when the key card would become demagnetized, or when the clients didn't know how to use the new devices and had to be taught how they worked whenever they registered at the desk.

As early as September 1988, Antonio was invited to SMAU, the prestigious New Technology Fair held in Milan. A roundtable discussion was held on what was new in technology related to the hotel sector, and the very young Antonio was one of the speakers. He described what they had done and how it worked. He was sincere when he spoke, and didn't hide the fact that technology required patience and trust. "You always have to believe in it," he said. "At first you feel like giving up and going back to using traditional systems."

The guests also had to be trained. Some of them had never even seen a magnetic hotel room key card. They would take it, go up to the room, and stand in front of the door without knowing what to do. They would then go back downstairs complaining that they hadn't been given the keys. The bolder guests would insert the card but forget to extract it. They thought that an automatic mechanism would give it back to them in the manner of an ATM machine. The door would thus stay locked, and the card stuck inside. Again the hotel guest would go down to the reception desk to complain that the system wasn't working. So a "trial stage" was required, but how gratifying to know that the hotel could offer such an innovative service! Since then, season after season, the hotels of the Zacchera Hotels company have been modernized, introducing new technology. The speech Antonio gave at the SMAU trade fair ended with a round of applause from all of the people working in the hotel business. Everyone knew that the future had come. As always, in the Zacchera household, it had come slightly faster than for others.

Carlo Zacchera and his wife, Margherita Silvera.

NEW TRAVELERS AT THE TURN OF THE MILLENNIUM

C arlo Zacchera loved to read. His desk was always covered with international magazines. He knew how to travel with his imagination while staying in one place. He had envisioned the Grand Hotel Dino without ever actually seeing anything like it, and with the help of his family he had made it come true. Everyone saw him as the wise visionary who could foretell the future, with the strength and the skill to make it come true. But even now that it was his competitors who read articles about him and learned from his actions, Carlo Zacchera continued to study and dream, to fill sheets of paper with numbers and sketches for plans.

Upon arriving early in the morning his children would find photocopies of articles on his desk. They were the stories of families who had lost their sense of unity. At times Carlo would add a note to remind his kids that the family is the most important thing. Whatever the hotels might become, he would say, they had to remain a common good: a home to be shared with the patrons, the guests. A big hotel resembles a city that is constantly changing. It can't simply stay still; it must change with each season. Like a ship that never stops sailing even when it is moored at the port. Carlo never wanted to close the hotels during the winter season. For many years he managed to avoid doing so by exploiting the proximity to Malpensa Airport. The crews and passengers in transit always needed a place to stay. But the winter—every winter—was also a time for renewal. Long months of what seemed like inactivity when the hotels were transformed to offer something new the following season.

The building site of the Grand Hotel Dino had not as yet closed when new works were begun in the other locations. The first of these was the Bristol in Stresa, right at the start of the decade, which saw the remodeling of all two hundred rooms.

This was followed by the Splendid, where air-conditioning was installed for the first time. That, too, was an innovation that resulted from Carlo's foresight. His brother Aldo, as ever a bit grouchy, had complained, trying to say that it would have taken a huge amount of work and that the guests would have returned even if they had left everything as it was, that no one used air-conditioning at the time. But Carlo read, and he traveled even when he was standing still. He knew that international tourism and the convention world were always on the lookout for new facilities. Air-conditioning was like a gust of wind: soon it would cross the ocean to cool the houses and the offices of the old continent. In the end, though, Aldo supervised the works. If that was what Carlo believed, then it was the right thing to do. He would have done anything for his brother and it all made even more sense because it was done within the family, and for the family. Also included as members of the family were the historic collaborators, without whom nothing would have been possible. And the guests were like members of the family as well, people for whom everything was conceived and carried out. In the Zacchera household, the art of hospitality was expressed as a form of collective intelligence, within the circular dimension of life.

In the mid-1990s, a vast renovation and upgrading of the Simplon began. The hotel was completely stripped bare, leaving just the load-bearing walls to testify to what the building had once been. The systems were renovated, as were the interiors, air-conditioning was added, of course, and there were twenty-five new rooms. Only a few months, four at most, to empty out, demolish, rebuild. Not like before, better than before. And then the look of surprise on the guests' faces as the final judgment. Proof that the ship had not stopped sailing.

Less than five years after the last work had been done, a new building site was also opened at the Hotel Bristol in Stresa, in order to create an underground garage. It was a futuristic structure at the time, considering the tight schedule and the proximity of the lake, which made any work below the ground a bold undertaking. It was sort of like tickling the great body of water that had been excavated by a glacier in prehistoric times.

The Magic
of Lake Orta, Mergozzo,
and Their Valleys

Lake Orta. Island of San Giulio.

Orta San Giulio. Piazza Motta and the Palazzotto.

Sacro Monte di Orta.

Lake Orta. Church of San Filiberto in Alzo, Pella.

The historical district of Omegna.

Mountain biking on the slopes of the Mottarone.

Mergozzo.

Orta and view of the Island of San Giulio.

In the Zacchera household, the art
of hospitality was expressed
as a form of collective intelligence,
in the circular dimension of life.

Also on the subject of water, for centuries generations of women had done their
laundry on the lakeshore. That was how Maria, Felicina, Maddalena, and Mariuccia
had washed Albergo Ristorante Italia's tablecloths and linens. The Zacchera family, which was always one step ahead of the times, had now created an industrial
laundry dedicated to internal services. It could have been used for laundry in other
businesses as well, but it remained limited to the family. At first it seemed huge,
but Carlo knew it would never be enough. It worked in the shadows, in the underground level of the Simplon. None of the guests ever visited it, yet it was one of the
few facilities of its kind in Italy. Hardly any hotel could count on an internal washing and pressing service. And each season, just like the hotel, the laundry would be
improved by adding new machinery and an organization that became increasingly
organized and efficient.

Everything was moving along smoothly, navigating at sight along the strategic
routes that had been charted by Carlo. The management of a hotel forces you to always move along the razor's edge, holding on tight to the air: imagining long-term
development plans and resolving unexpected everyday problems. In every instant,
in the life of a hotel, something unexpected can happen.

Carlo was in command on the deck of the ship, together with his siblings. Always
elegant, patient, his black tie perfectly knotted. His wife Margherita had become a
crucial figure: the Hotel Bristol in Stresa was her brainchild. Francesco Zacchera was
the director, but he traveled a lot for work. He loved liaising with people, he was kind
to everyone. He had a noble air about him, dressed in a jacket, with a white shirt and
cufflinks, even in summer. He had a kind thought for everyone and was very tender
with the children. He knew how to smile at people, a rare quality. But the management
of the hotel was a wholly feminine task, with Margherita at the reception desk, along
with their daughter Gabriella, who had graduated from hotel management school
and spent her childhood and teenage years in that hotel. "We always got along,"
Gabriella remembers today. "She was special, unique, and very good at her work and
determined, but I knew how to deal with her. I would do what she asked and add
something of my own, which our mother appreciated, all of us complicit."

During the winter season Margherita worked with her husband and helped him to shape new ideas. She shared every strategic matter with him and made his dreams come true, his visions clearer. She also knew how to be bold when managing the reservations. She handled them confidently because she always knew what was going on in the other hotels, and how to transfer the guests from one hotel to another. It was a sort of roulette, which would soon become a full-fledged booking system, perfected in a very sophisticated way by their son Antonio. In the family's eyes, the hotels of the Zacchera Hotels company were already interchangeable structures. Each of them had their own personality, something special that attracted a certain type of clientele. But they were also a series of rooms that could be used as communicating vessels. One big family of hotels. Buildings like people, who must learn to be together so that their common patrimony will never be lost, but be preserved and prized instead.

In this expanded vision of the people who inhabit the common spaces of life and work, the role of the staff was crucial. While it is true that the Zaccheras had focused on the client, without the collaborators nothing would have been possible. They knew everything about the hotels: they had worked in every department ever since they were children and their skill underpinned the professional relations. In the evening Carlo would often be the one emptying the ashtrays. Whenever a person expressed amazement, he would shrug and say that no one likes going to someone's home to find dust swept away under the carpet. He would never have wanted a guest to reproach him for being careless.

Hospitality is an art that calls for passion, devotion, total involvement. When a problem arises, you have to be there, ready to solve it. "You're happy to take on every responsibility," admits Andrea Zacchera, who now runs the convention department. "You're not sure why you do it, but you saw your parents, your grandparents doing the same thing. You can't even imagine behaving differently." Responsibilities can weigh you down, but some people know how to bear them casually, almost lightly. Sister Gabriella has inherited their mother's spirit and has become, together with her brothers, a point of reference for the clients as well as for the staff. Whatever day it is, whatever the season, her smile brightens the life that is going on in the Zacchera Hotels. Kindness toward the guests becomes an everyday, spontaneous, and generous gesture. "Problems are often an opportunity for getting together and talking," Gabriella adds. As always, with a smile.

When the decade drew to a close, it was time to renovate the Hotel Dino as well. Aldo didn't agree and had tried to put off the renovation work. He was a big man, with a very big heart. He was often irritable, and if he didn't agree with something it was impossible not to know so. From that point of view, he was like an open book, a simple man whose feelings were easily apparent.

The idea for reinvigorating the new hotel had especially been that of Antonio, Carlo's firstborn son. Together they had discussed the opportunity to redo the interiors of a block of rooms and to work on the design of the common areas. The ground floor had been completely renovated, with reception services, offices, convention rooms. On the fourth floor, new suites and executive rooms were added, which still today are among the most prestigious on Lake Maggiore. And then, after the positive experience of the Bristol, a large underground garage was built, enough for over three hundred vehicles. The tight schedule and being so close to the water had complicated the work. But in the end the building site manager had finished the job before the new season could begin.

Massimo Zacchera, Carlo's son, had been working alongside Uncle Aldo for years to manage the construction and maintenance works. Also working with him was his cousin Paolo, Mariuccia's son, who later became an engineer. "Even when we were kids, we really liked going to the building sites," they both recall. "To see how things that had been conceived, and often only imagined, were actually made!"

This time Aldo stayed away from the construction site. Although he had spent his life surrounded by the rubble of construction, he refused to oversee the new intervention. He thought it was unnecessary, and when he got angry, he was a force to be reckoned with. He was a big man. But after all the scaffolding had been removed, he paid his compliments to Antonio. Because the work had been done well, and because Antonio had the courage to complete it against his uncle's will. Aldo acknowledged that Antonio had done an exceptional job.

The new millennium began in the worst of ways, with a devastating natural catastrophe. The flood of 2000 brought the entire region to its knees, as had already happened in 1993. Based on that previous experience, special barriers had been created to stop the water, and pumps had been prepared to empty out any places that might get flooded. But the large windows with a view of the lake that made the Grand Hotel Dino so unique proved to be a disaster. It had been raining for days on end and the water level of the lake had risen dangerously high. The disaster occurred suddenly, while the hotel was filled with guests and a convention was underway. The water had overflowed its natural basin and entered the hotel after first filling up the underground garage. When water starts flowing it overruns everything. It entered the rooms like a fast-flowing river and filled them until they looked like swimming pools. The hotel was instantly evacuated. The siblings and cousins in the Zacchera family used boats to navigate the meeting rooms with the help of their collaborators, rescuing the chairs and tables that floated around there. It looked like they had been hit by a hurricane destroying everything. It was a harsh blow to the hotel and to the family. The Hotel Dino had just been renovated; everything was ready for another building site. It wasn't a question of improving it, however, but of bringing it back to life.

All the rooms had been flooded, and outside two of the spaces that had been dedicated to tennis could no longer be used. Carlo Zacchera took advantage of the situation for another one of his stunning insights. He would have the fields covered and turned into a new convention center sixteen-feet tall and almost 5,500 square feet across. "It became our most important convention room," says Massimo Zacchera. "We inaugurated it in September 2001 with Lucio Dalla in attendance. We call that room 'Ballroom Carlo,' in our father's memory."

The grand hotel stayed closed for the entire season and six more months working full-time were needed. Its perfect shape was restored, like an athlete who can compete again after having had an accident. But the flood had taken

Hospitality is an art that calls for passion, devotion, total involvement. When a problem arises, you have to be there, ready to solve it.

with it the man who had wanted that hotel more than anyone else. The athlete had returned, but the trainer was gone.

Carlo Zacchera had always been slightly superstitious. He feared the numbers thirteen and seventeen. He died of a heart attack the night of May 13, 2001. Dino had also died on that day. The number thirteen that kept on coming back also seemed to symbolically underscore the indissoluble strength of their relationship. The tidal wave had already overrun Carlo's unstoppable energy, his optimism, his confident sense of calm. Perhaps that time he really did fear he wouldn't make it. The flood had destroyed him, along with the weight of his responsibilities, the hard work he had done over the years.

Life can be cruel, and two years later Aldo died as well. They had been more than brothers. Guardian angels, whose presence was enough to make sense of everything. Aldo died of a rare and sudden type of cancer and, just as had been the case when Annibale and Dino died, his presence was especially felt after he was gone. Now that they were gone, they were always there, with their children and grandchildren. Their shadows repeated Dino's words when he asked everyone to stay united. *Try always to love one another.*

Many people went to Carlo's funeral. People of all kinds, often ones the family did not know but whom Carlo had helped. It was not a surprise, but rather a further point of pride to see how much happiness he had sown along the way. He knew how to attach the right importance to things, and on his scale of values, even for a successful entrepreneur like himself, people's lives were more important than a financial statement. He knew how to dedicate himself to everyone with the same attention. Many famous industrialists and businessmen sought him out for advice, but there were also workers who talked to him about their health problems, their family concerns. Everything was important for Carlo Zacchera. He loved details, he hated superficiality. And when he interrupted a meeting, it was to accompany one of his grandchildren to school. He also knew how to see the hidden qualities in people. He encouraged collaborators who seemed unsuited to the task, finding the right job for everyone. He prized individuals, convinced that everyone had a special talent to express.

Talent is like a verb, transitive, conjugated in the future. It often remains hidden and hard to recognize. It's hard to single it out and you need to polish it like a precious stone, until it starts to shine. Patient, tenacious, almost obstinate work. Carlo Zacchera was a master at this.

As sometimes occurs in life, what nature destroys man manages to rebuild. Like before, often better than before. And this time as well, from the floodwater the Grand Hotel Dino resurfaced with a new underground tunnel that connected it to the Simplon, making the hotel complex of Baveno one of the largest structures in all of Italy: over five hundred rooms, and fifteen meeting rooms with a view of Lake Maggiore and the Borromean Islands.

This new project was also linked to the memory of Carlo Zacchera and to his ability to read the future. He had gotten the idea when the Town of Baveno had been forced to dig a tunnel to be able to work on the sewer system. He had taken advantage of the situation, offering to have the excavating done himself, on the condition that he would be allowed to dig a tunnel connecting the Simplon to the Dino.

In 2002, a high-end automobile manufacturer, Audi, would choose the Hotel Zacchera to organize an event for the launch of the new A8, the most prestigious car of the gamma. An event that would last more than a month, with hundreds of clients in transit between the two hotels. The idea of the underground tunnel was back in the news, with Carlo's plans and project almost completely brought to term. The tunnel was built in his memory, the way he would have wanted it. A long and elegant corridor, with dim lighting and paintings on the walls. A touch of elegance, to make the way it worked all the more special.

Today the Grand Hotel Dino and the Hotel Simplon are considered a single complex. Unique in its kind. And each time you go through that tunnel you breathe a little of the spirit of Carlo, Francesco, and Aldo. You hear the echo of their voices. Hotels are containers of stories. Their walls talk and they harbor tales. Emotions. Although they are no longer with us, the Zacchera brothers are still always there.

The building of the art gallery that connects the Grand Hotel Dino to the Hotel Simplon.

Flooding of Lake Maggiore, October 2000. Andrea and Paolo, in a boat inside the center for meetings.

POSTCARDS FROM THE FUTURE: EXCELLENCE BETWEEN VISION AND LANDSCAPE

"Father was always very good at stimulating us to do things," Andrea Zacchera recalls. "At first we entered on tiptoe, little by little, just to lend a hand. Then we found ourselves immersed in an activity that became our life." When the three brothers were gone, the management of the Zacchera group ended up in the safe hands of the fourth generation. Children and grandchildren had come together, each with their own skills, expressing their own talent.

Of course, at first it wasn't easy to replace Carlo: he alone did the work of many people. And for as long as he was the one doing the work, everything seemed easy. Handling his papers had made his value even more evident. Some people are irreplaceable. One can only try to keep them alive in one's memory and in what is taught to the successive generations. It is a lay form of immortality.

And so, continuing along the path that had been traced by the Zacchera brothers, the younger members of the family continued to open new building sites to shape new dreams. The art of hospitality that becomes the culture of the project, one season after another.

Toward the end of the first decade of the 2000s, while the world was undergoing a difficult economic crisis, both the Simplon and the Splendid hotels were renovated. In the latter hotel, the number of rooms for the guests was reduced to make more room, new convention rooms were created, and access to the lake was prioritized with one of the very few private beaches in the Baveno-Stresa area. The laundry in the basement of the Simplon was relocated outside, and it became a high point, based on the most modern, technologically advanced, and sustainable criteria, with the recycling of 80 percent of the water. In the spaces that were freed from the previous structure new rooms were made to enrich a convention system that was already unique, surrounded by a natural landscape without equal.

Altogether, Zacchera Hotels has about a thousand rooms available, and a modular system of meeting rooms managed with the most cutting-edge technology. But this too was a difficult conquest. The fruit of hard decisions to make, shared ideas, and projects carried out with passion and determination. Investing with faith in the future, even when the present was concerning.

A glimpse of the Hotel Simplon garden.

As mentioned before, one of the first innovations in the Zacchera Hotels was the air-conditioning. The heat pumps that fueled the conditioners of the Grand Hotel Dino were as long as railway cars and occupied entire underground spaces below the hotel. The system drew water from the lake so that, by circulating, it cooled off the heat pumps. Although the system worked well, the costs were very high. The idea of a new, simpler, and more efficient system was the result of a mistake. It became clear that the water could be circulated directly in the system and serve as a cooling element. Today it is drawn from the depth of the lake at a constant temperature of 44.6 degrees farenheit; then, a plate heat exchanger is used to exchange it with the water in the internal circuit; lastly, it returns to its natural basin. A simple, economical system that exploits a resource in the region without affecting the environment. "We are proud of this solution," Antonio Zacchera says. "It's a good thing that our lake can offer us such a precious resource. Otherwise, it would not be possible." And yet a brilliant solution such as this continues to be the only example on the lake. Sustainable air-conditioning, achieved without having to use gas, remains a distinguishing feature of the Zacchera Hotels.

Technological innovation was Carlo's focus, and its legacy was taken up by his son Antonio. After being ahead of the times by using magnetic key cards and the digitization of the rooms, Antonio pushed to make hotels that were increasingly evolved. Buildings so complex that technology can hardly ever be acquired in packages defined by others, but must always somehow be developed within, based on needs. The need for a new management software often emerges from the need to resolve a problem. When, for instance, the kitchen requested new recycling bins, Antonio became curious and decided to study the subject. He watched over the department for a period of time and seen many examples of inefficiency in product management. The first thing that needed to be done was to develop a labeling system for the food that included delivery and expiry dates.

Nowadays, everything is recorded and the kitchen has a dedicated program that in real-time updates the ingredients used for each preparation, taking

The fourth generation of the Zacchera family:
Andrea, Raffaele, Antonio, Paolo, Enrico, Anna Maria,
Maria Gabriella, Mamma Margherita, and Massimo.

Zacchera Hotels has been
a member of the Italian
Historical Brands Association
since 2022.

Sketch of the cooling and air-conditioning
system at the Grand Hotel Dino, Baveno.

into consideration the season and nationality of the guest, and providing information on what is left over. Each recipe, even the most creative one, is based on a solid management architecture that avoids waste and makes it possible to plan acquisitions beforehand, without being impacted by the sudden lack of raw material. Even the collaboration with charity organizations that offer meals to the needy is based on the in-depth knowledge of the products in the warehouse. The fight against waste and for social sustainability are two important thresholds that have been reached. Further ways of seeking quality. Planning, in order to be free to create.

Another technological innovation involved equipping all the people working in the rooms with a tablet. When it was first introduced in 2015 it seemed like madness for all the housekeepers to have carts equipped with a support for a small portable computer. "But when an entrepreneur has a vision," Antonio Zacchera says, "he has to believe in it all the way. To be able to implement his idea he needs to be stubborn, determined, and patient. Often, you don't get the results immediately."

The staff assigned to clean the rooms were the first to look at the new device with suspicion. It had been decided to try the idea in the most difficult situation: in the almost four hundred rooms of the Grand Hotel Dino. If it could work there, it could work everywhere. The system did work, but some of the staff resisted using it.

It was above all Gabriella who made it easy to introduce change. She would talk to the staff, share their concerns and their fears. But she had faith in her brother's vision and she knew that with a bit of effort and some good will, all of them together would achieve excellent results. At one point there was an Internet outage, and it was one of the older, more expert collaborators who complained on behalf of her coworkers that without a tablet they simply couldn't work!

This is often the case with new technology: at first, you're nostalgic about the past, but then you can't do without what's new. The tablet collected all the data concerning the rooms and allowed them to communicate with other management units, from the kitchen to the laundry to maintenance. Each environment was visualized on the screen of the device that photographed in real-time the state of the room and what, if anything, was needed. A burnt-out light bulb was immediately communicated to the maintenance department. And the guest's name was on the tablet, so the staff member in charge of cleaning could address him or her the same way someone working at reception would. From the little things to the big ones, the diffused management system became a new ally that allowed for the quality to be improved overall, offering services that were more exclusive and personalized.

The program that assembles all this data and puts it into a single, large digital hub did not exist and could not but be developed internally. Over the years, an integrated system was devised drawn up specifically for hotel management, personalized based on the needs of Zacchera Hotels. It is interesting to note how hotel software has to be both sophisticated and simple, intuitive and solid. These are work tools, used every day by dozens, hundreds of collaborators, often seasonal workers from other countries. Everything has to be immediate and effective. As Carlo Zacchera would often say, the real challenge is making hard things easy.

Another amazing innovation that Zacchera Hotels offers is a program that makes it possible to configure and create in 3D the way the convention and dining rooms are set up. This time as well it all happened more or less by chance. The presentation by a supplier intrigued Antonio Zacchera and his brother Andrea. It introduced an app that allowed you to visualize different types of faucets and to assemble them in multiple virtual configurations.

"Can this be done with large rooms, too?" Antonio had asked.

"I think so, but you have to talk to the programmer."

"I'd like to meet him."

The creator of the app was an enthusiastic, brilliant young man. Antonio spoke to him about his idea of making something that instead of faucets would allow you to combine entire arrangements in convention and dining rooms.

"In theory it can be done," he said, "except that it never has been done before."

"Well, then, you'll be the first!"

> When an entrepreneur has a vision, he has to believe in it all the way. To be able to implement his idea, he needs to be stubborn, determined, and patient.

And so they set to work. It was a question of starting from the plans for the rooms that needed to be transformed into 3D models. After that, all the possible combinations of the arrangements had to be realized, photographed, and then all the various components had to be modeled. Antonio wanted to develop a program that would allow for the creation of full-fledged high-definition sets. These would be very useful when deciding together with the client the type of setup they wanted, but it would also help to put them in a better position than the competition. Today the program is in full use and allows for the generation of over a million possible combinations.

"It was a very hard task," Andrea Zacchera admits, "but now we can manage all the arrangements. We're always one step ahead, in terms of both the programming and the realization of the events."

Each year, in the trade fairs, the customers and the competitors want to see what's new at the Zacchera group, and almost always these are highly technological novelties.

A century and a half has passed since the Osteria Milanese was founded. The Zacchera group has become a complex reality, while still holding on to its family dimension. Just as it was in the early days, the hotel is a home, the clients are guests. Welcoming them is an art, a vocation, whether we are dealing with large companies or small families. The group philosophy continues along the line defined by its founding fathers, and is based on a dual managerial register: on the one hand, structures that are totally free to resolve specific problems; on the other, strategic choices that are always linked to the general direction.

All of the group's realities are one big infrastructure that intercepts flows of people. It influences the development of the region and it accepts, for its own growth, the drive of the region itself. Each hotel has its own story and its own image, but everything must always refer to the identity of business.

Other Lake Maggiore hoteliers, albeit prestigious, move in a less structured way. What is missing is a system that comes with an associative spirit, a general philosophy that makes it possible for the entire area to bestow personality and

Just as it was in the early days, the hotel is a home, the clients are guests. Welcoming them is an art, a vocation, whether we are dealing with large companies or small families.

character on the tourist hoteliers. Unlike the competition, the services offered by Zacchera group are always personalized and maintain the warmth that remains the family's legacy, handed down from one generation to the next since the mid-nineteenth century.

At the heart of the entire organization is the figure of the client, without whom nothing would make any sense. The client who decides to use the Zacchera group first of all chooses the quality of a company that always calls into play its own credibility and reputation. For every hotelier, these are the most important tokens. A style that is perfected by work over time. An experience developed since childhood, when work and play, public and private life were combined.

In the hotels of the Zacchera group the most ambitious projects are always carefully matched to the details. As when Carlo Zacchera used to empty out the ashtrays. An outer cleanliness that reflected an inner one, a clarity of ideas, a rectitude of thought. These, too, are precious tokens.

The recent pandemic was like another flood, except that it was longer and had more victims. Hotels remained closed for almost two years, and the concerns undermined certainties that seemed consolidated. But in spite of the difficulties, the group's strategic line never changed. The investments never ceased, and the stakes in the convention sector never lost. It is likely that companies will need even more moments of dialogue and in-person meetings to redress the hours of work done from home. The hotel will become an increasingly physical place where people will be able to exchange information and emotions. The space of the encounter, of the ideas that are shared at the peripheries of the meetings, at the café counter, at the swimming pool border, while taking a trip to the lake. Of course, the new hygiene regulations have required safety standards that differ from the ones in the past, but for companies like the Zacchera Group these restrictions have been yet another opportunity to continue to improve.

Already over the past two years, when openings were limited, the group acquired an "ISO 45005 certificate" against contamination by pathogenic agents. It adopted safety protocols that were even tougher than those set by the rules.

The Colors and Scents
of the Most Beautiful Gardens
in the World, Arona, and the
Statue of San Carlo Borromeo

Isola Bella. The terraced gardens.

One of the peacocks on Isola Madre.

Stresa. Villa Pallavicino.

Borromean Gulf.

Verbania. Villa Taranto, the vat filled with lotus flowers.

Arona. The lakeshore with a statue of the Boatsman and Angera Fortress.

Arona. Statue of San Carlo Borromeo.

Equipment was installed to sanitize common rooms and bedrooms, along with pedal hand-sanitizer dispensers. This line of rigorous behavior consists of gestures that are not meant to be alarming, but should, rather, offer a feeling of security.

The Zacchera group is now celebrating its one hundred and fiftieth anniversary. Over a thousand rooms and more than fifty convention rooms make up a small city that is born and reborn each day on the shores of Lake Maggiore. Managing and administering it wisely is a mission more than a job. The Zaccheras have become master artisans of hospitality. They see welcoming as a fine product, and in their everyday work, they express the soul of the region. "We live in an earthly paradise," Massimo Zacchera admits with satisfaction. "Every morning before going to work I go to the town square and I get the newspaper. I see the sun rise, and I can't help but take a picture of it. The day starts well."

A unique landscape, the opposite of haste: the calm of the lake, the mountains reflected in the water, the wind that caresses the birds in flight, and the princely dwellings like Palazzo Borromeo. Thickly wooded forests and rivers, marble and granite quarries, islands cradled by the Mediterranean climate that allows citrus plants to ripen at the foot of the Alps, exotic plants that reminded Joséphine Bonaparte of the gardens in Martinique. All this is Baveno, Stresa, Lake Maggiore. And when you look at how the greatest hotels in the world are ranked according to the number of rooms and what is available for conventions, you find the most prestigious ones to be located in London, Paris, and Madrid. Followed by Baveno. If you've never come here before you will think there must be some mistake. You'll take a look at a map and discover that a place with that name really does exist.

And when you come here once, you will definitely return.
And when you come back once, at least in your heart, you'll never leave again.

LET YOURSELF
BE WELCOMED

T he story of the Zacchera family crosses the generations and is set in the landscape of Lake Maggiore. A natural amphitheater, created in prehistoric times by the movement of the glaciers. Availed with masses of water and mountains, nature was then able to make a miracle. "The most enchanting place in the world," wrote Montesquieu. "The soul is surprised by this picturesque contrast ... After overcoming cliffs and arid landscapes, one finds oneself in fairy-tale-like places."

The mild Mediterranean climate, the constant alternation between lowlands and reliefs, gentle meadows, and sharp rock formations: a pictorial enchantment of high and low, dark and light, like some Baroque triumph. A unique and inimitable context, which has inspired the hand of man in the construction of villas and gardens that have greeted the most illustrious visitors.

Zacchera Hotels, on the lakeshore between Baveno and Stresa, have for over a century and a half hosted travelers from all around the world and guided them, like an interior compass. From here the view stretches far beyond the horizon.

Naturally, the Borromeo Islands are the heart of it all, absolute gems set in the lake. They are like precious stones, moored to an imaginary pier that joins them to the coast. Expanding to the west are steep chestnut, larch, and beech forests, that rise up toward the slopes of the Mottarone: thick forests that like a green mantle cover the pink granite. To the north is the valley of the Toce and the Ossola, the treasure trove of Candoglia marble quarries, the only marble that is used for Milan Cathedral. To the east, past the Swiss end of the lake, the coast becomes impervious, and the hermitage of Santa Caterina del Sasso symbolizes this corner of Verbano, a place of tranquility that dominates from another rocky spur. Lastly, to the south is the corridor of the Ticino, overseen by the Rocca di Angera, a splendid medieval castle with frescoes and decorations inside. This fortress is the military and political expression of the Borromeo family, while the Islands that caress the coastline are its gentler soul: the precious gift of nature's generosity.

The entities of Zacchera Hotels are witnesses to these regions and their stories, the point of arrival and departure, the fundamental heart of journeys that involve the senses and the mind before the body. These are significant places, where each client is truly a guest. Let us discover them, one by one, via the evocative force of the images.

Verbania. Villa Taranto, the terraced gardens.

Isola Bella.

A VIEW OF THE BORROMEAN ISLANDS

THE ROOMS WITH A VIEW
AT THE GRAND HOTEL DINO

G rand Hotel Dino is a hotel named after a person. It is a welcoming, exclusive place, dedicated to the memory of Corrado (Dino) Zacchera. Overlooking the placid waters of Lake Maggiore, it is reflected in the beauty of the Borromean Islands. Places where the search for harmony has become a philosophy of life. This prestigious hotel is born from a clear vision of the future. Digital technology is vital to an integrated system of meeting rooms lit by natural lighting, immersed in the green of a luxuriant garden, with a pool and a private beach.

It is a completely new way of conceiving business meetings as opportunities for encounter, moments of individual and collective growth. The Grand Hotel Dino offers ambience and services that modify the perception of time. Harmony and equilibrium of activity dedicated to oneself, family, and work.

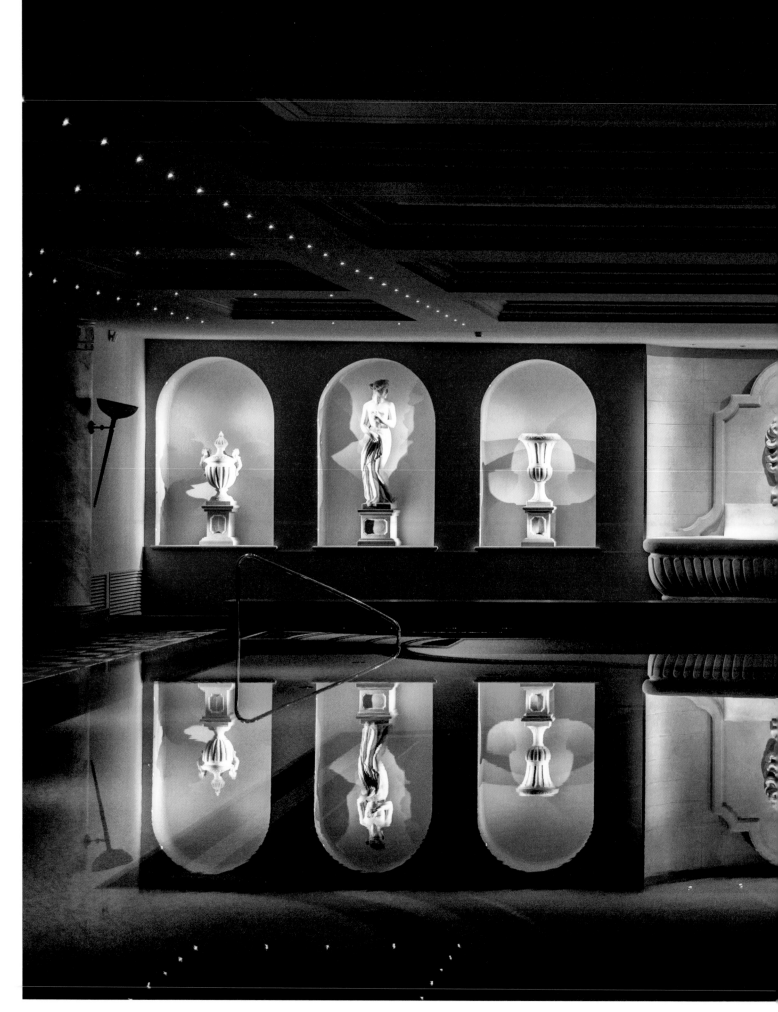

THE STRESA
LAKESHORE

THE ELEGANCE OF THE
GRAND HOTEL BRISTOL

G rand Hotel Bristol preserves the exclusive charm of the aristocratic palazzo. Of the original Villa Mercedes it has maintained the noble character and the Baroque decor inserted in a centuries-old park overlooking Lake Maggiore. Stresa has forever been the piece of land closest to the Borromean Islands. From the Bristol's terraces one can capture unforgettable views of Isola Bella, with its Renaissance villa and Italian-style garden. The gaze reaches as far as the coastline of Isola dei Pescatori, where the Zacchera family was born; lastly, our eyes take in Isola Madre, whose nature is so lush it reminds you of Joséphine de Beauharnais—Napoleon's wife and a native of Martinique. Hotel Bristol welcomes its guests in a prestigious context conducive to fostering relationships between people, stimulating the encounter between ideas and cultures. For over half a century it has received people from around Europe and every other corner of the world. Loyal guests who, once they have discovered this corner of paradise, never leave it again.

A SMALL PIAZZA
ON THE LAKE

—

HOTEL SPLENDID
AND ITS VIEW
OF THE WATER

H otel Splendid is the hotel where everything was born. This was the location of the Osteria Milanese, the Albergo Ristorante Italia and, with the expansion, the Nouvel Hotel Italie, currently the Hotel Splendid. A building that over the course of one hundred and fifty years of history has preserved an intimate and familiar dimension. The image of Hotel Splendid as a "small piazza on the lake" expresses the more genuine dimension of the Zacchera family: the art of hospitality in the unique and unparalleled context of Lake Maggiore. Even the smallest detail expresses the original spirit of adventure. From the rooms to the pool, from the restaurant to the garden, from the reception to the private beach, everything conveys the determination to make a dream come true. Hotel Splendid encompasses the untiring desire to look to the future, while walking in the footsteps of the forebears. A soft line that follows the curves of the lake, where the dawns and dusks mark the passing of the days.

THE BREATH OF
A CENTURIES-OLD PARK

—

THE SIMPLON
AND ITS GARDEN

D uring the war, Hotel Simplon was a hospital. Still today— transformed into a prestigious hotel—it has confirmed its natural vocation to care for people. Each detail is aimed at the guests' well-being, starting from the majestic park with rare nature and centuries-old plants, where everyone can find their personal equilibrium and well-being. Nature as a symbol of harmony and perfection. A precious gift to offer the guests. Carlo Zacchera and his family lived in an apartment in Hotel Simplon, the headquarters of the Group's business. The clients are never considered mere tourists, but rather as loyal guests, whom the entire staff know by name. Life at Hotel Simplon flows harmoniously, smoothly. Like a handmade, bespoke outfit always to be worn casually.

FROM THE WATER OF THE LAKE TO THE EMBRACE OF THE ALPS

A RELAXING STAY AT THE CARL & DO

F or the Zacchera family, the Carl & Do residence is like a fifth child, the name formed by joining the names of Carlo and Aldo Zacchera. It is an innovative structure capable of combining the reception of the Grand Hotel with the freedom and warmth of a private residence. The guests are families who come from all over Europe to discover the beauties of Lake Maggiore. The landscape here is unique, a treasure trove of wonders to be enjoyed slowly, with all the freedom desired. Those who choose the Carl & Do residence always enjoy the privilege of being the guest of honor, free to move about without the restrictions of time and space, to decide on the pace of their stay. From the lake water to the mountain peaks, there are no limits to one's emotions. Certain to return, after every adventure, to the warm embrace of a home that is as exclusive as a hotel.

Photo Credits

All photographs, courtesy of Archivio Zacchera except page 28
© The History Collection / Alamy / IPA

© Paolo Beltrami: 148–149
© Maurizio Besana: 76–77
© Sara Bovio: 124
© Foto Pessina Domodossola: 112, 134–135, 144
© Dario Fusaro: 120, 174–175, 180–181, 200–201
© Piero Gatti 4–5, 6–7, 38–39, 42–43, 44–45, 48, 98–99, 100–101, 106–107, 138–139
© Andrea Lazzarini / Scenari srl Stresa: 16, 24, 50, 53, 56, 82, 84
© Andrea Marcovicchio / Studio 1013: 166–167, 178–179, 188–189, 196, 204–205
© Katie May: cover, 10, 162–163, 208–209, 212–213, 214–215
© Giancarlo Parazzoli: 66–67, 68–69, 70–71, 78–79, 130–131
© Strixia.com: 152–153, 154–155, 170–171, 182, 184–185, 202–203
© Trippini Stampe Antiche, www.trippini.it: 21, 27, 30, 31

The Publisher may be contacted by entitled parties
for any iconographic sources that have not been identified.

Art Direction and Layout
Greta Heartfelt

English Translation
Sylvia Adrian Notini

Iconographical Research
Marina Itolli

© 2023 Mondadori Libri S.p.A.
Distributed in English throughout the World
by Rizzoli International Publications Inc.
300 Park Avenue South
New York, NY 10010, USA

ISBN: 978-88-918370-7-3

2024 2025 2026 2027 / 10 9 8 7 6 5 4 3 2 1

First edition: March 2024

This volume was printed at Errestampa S.r.l.
Via Portico 27, Orio al Serio, Bergamo
Printed in Italy

Visit us online:
Facebook.com/RizzoliNewYork
Twitter: @Rizzoli_Books
Instagram.com/RizzoliBooks
Pinterest.com/RizzoliBooks
Youtube.com/user/RizzoliNY
Issuu.com/Rizzoli